THE KINGDOM OF GOD
AND HISTORY

VOLUME III
The Official
Oxford Conference
Books

THE OFFICIAL OXFORD CONFERENCE BOOKS

1. **THE CHURCH AND ITS FUNCTION IN SOCIETY**
by Dr. W. A. Visser 't Hooft and Dr. J. H. Oldham

2. **THE CHRISTIAN UNDERSTANDING OF MAN**
by Prof. T. E. Jessop, Prof. R. L. Calhoun, Prof. N. N. Alexeiev, Prof. Emil Brunner, Pastor Pierre Maury, the Rev. Austin Farrer, Prof. W. M. Horton

3. **THE KINGDOM OF GOD AND HISTORY**
by Prof. C. H. Dodd, Dr. Edwyn Bevan, Dr. Christopher Dawson, Prof. Eugene Lyman, Prof. Paul Tillich, Prof. H. Wendland, Prof. H. G. Wood

4. **CHRISTIAN FAITH AND THE COMMON LIFE**
by Nils Ehrenström, Prof. M. Dibelius, Prof. John Bennett, The Archbishop of York, Prof. Reinhold Niebuhr, Prof. H. H. Farmer, Dr. W. Wiesner

5. **CHURCH AND COMMUNITY**
by Prof. E. E. Aubrey, Prof. E. Barker, Dr. Björkquist, Dr. H. Lilje, Prof. S. Zankov, Dr. Paul Douglass, Prof. K. S. Latourette, M. Boegner

6. **CHURCH, COMMUNITY, AND STATE IN RELATION TO EDUCATION**
by Prof. F. Clarke, Dr. Paul Monroe, Prof. W. Zenkovsky, C. R. Morris, J. W. D. Smith, " X," Prof. Ph. Kohnstamm, J. H. Oldham

7. **THE UNIVERSAL CHURCH AND THE WORLD OF NATIONS**
by the Marquess of Lothian, Sir Alfred Zimmern, Dr. O. von der Gablentz, John Foster Dulles, Prof. Max Huber, Pastor W. Menn, the Rev. V. A. Demant, Prof. Otto Piper, Canon C. E. Raven

THE OXFORD CONFERENCE: Official Report
Including the full text of the reports issued by the five sections of the Conference, Oxford, England, 1937. With an introduction by J. H. Oldham

WORLD CHAOS OR WORLD CHRISTIANITY
A popular interpretation of Oxford and Edinburgh, 1937
by Henry Smith Leiper

THE KINGDOM OF GOD AND HISTORY

by

H. G. WOOD

C. H. DODD

EDWYN BEVAN

EUGENE LYMAN

PAUL TILLICH

H. D. WENDLAND

CHRISTOPHER DAWSON

WILLETT, CLARK & COMPANY

CHICAGO   NEW YORK

1938

CONTENTS

GENERAL INTRODUCTION

FEW will question the significance of the issues which engaged the attention of the conference on Church, Community, and State held at Oxford in July, 1937. More important than the conference itself is the continuing process, in
which the conference was not more than an incident, of an
attempt on the part of the Christian churches collectively
— without, up to the present, the official participation of
the Church of Rome, but not without the unofficial help
of some of its thinkers and scholars [1] — to understand the
true nature of the vital conflict between the Christian faith
and the secular and pagan tendencies of our time, and to
see more clearly the responsibilities of the church in relation to the struggle. What is at stake is the future of Christianity. The Christian foundations of western civilization
have in some places been swept away and are everywhere
being undermined. The struggle today concerns those
common assumptions regarding the meaning of life without which, in some form, no society can cohere. These
vast issues are focussed in the relation of the church to the
state and to the community, because the non-Christian
forces of today are tending more and more to find embodiment in an all-powerful state, committed to a particular
philosophy of life and seeking to organize the whole of life
in accordance with a particular doctrine of the end of
man's existence, and in an all-embracing community life

[1] A volume of papers by Roman Catholic writers dealing with subjects
closely akin to the Oxford Conference and stimulated in part by the preparatory work for Oxford will be published shortly under the title *Die
Kirche Christi: ihre heilende, gestaltende und ordnende Kraft für den
Menschen und seine Welt.*

vii

which claims to be at once the source and the goal of all human activities: a state, that is to say, which aims at being also a church.

To aid in the understanding of these issues the attempt was made in preparation for the conference at Oxford to enlist as many as possible of the ablest minds in different countries in a common effort to think out some of the major questions connected with the theme of the conference. During the three years preceding the conference studies were undertaken wider in their range and more thorough in their methods than any previous effort of a similar kind on the part of the Christian churches. This was made possible by the fact that the Universal Christian Council for Life and Work, under whose auspices the conference was held, possessed a department of research at Geneva with two full-time directors and was also able, in view of the conference, to establish an office in London with two full-time workers and to set up an effective agency for the work of research in America. There was thus provided the means of circulating in mimeographed form (in many instances in three languages) a large number of papers for comment, of carrying on an extensive and continuous correspondence, and of maintaining close personal touch with many leading thinkers and scholars in different countries.

Intensive study over a period of three years was devoted to nine main subjects. The results of this study are embodied in the six volumes to which this general introduction relates and in two others. The plan and contents of each, and most of the papers, were discussed in at least two or three small international conferences or groups. The contributions were circulated in first draft to a number of critics in different countries and comments were received often from as many as thirty or forty persons. Nearly all the papers were revised, and in some instances entirely rewritten, in the light of these criticisms.

Both the range of the contributions and the fact that the papers have taken their present shape as the result of a wide international interchange of ideas give these books an ecumenical character which marks a new approach to the subjects with which they deal. They thus provide an opportunity such as has hardly existed before for the study in an ecumenical context of some of the grave and pressing problems which today concern the Christian church throughout the world.

The nine subjects to which preparatory study was devoted were the following:

1. The Christian Understanding of Man.
2. The Kingdom of God and History.
3. Christian Faith and the Common Life.
4. The Church and Its Function in Society.
5. Church and Community.
6. Church and State.
7. Church, Community and State in Relation to the Economic Order.
8. Church, Community and State in Relation to Education.
9. The Universal Church and the World of Nations.

The last six of these subjects were considered at the Oxford Conference, and the reports prepared by the sections into which the conference was divided will be found in the official report of the conference entitled *The Oxford Conference, Official Report.* (Willett, Clark & Company).

A volume on *The Church and its Function in Society,* by Dr. W. A. Visser 't Hooft and Dr. J. H. Oldham (Willett, Clark & Company), was published prior to the conference.

Three of the volumes in the present series of six have to

do with the first three subjects in the list already given. These are fundamental issues which underlie the study of all the other subjects. The titles of these volumes are:

The Christian Understanding of Man.
The Kingdom of God and History.
The Christian Faith and the Common Life.

The remaining three volumes in the series are a contribution to the study of three of the main subjects considered by the Oxford Conference. These are:

Church and Community.
Church, Community and State in Relation to Education.
The Universal Church and the World of Nations.

The subject of church and state is treated in a book by Mr. Nils Ehrenström, one of the directors of the research department. This has been written in the light of discussions in several international conferences and groups and of a wide survey of the relevant literature, and has been published under the title *Christian Faith and the Modern State* (Willett, Clark & Company).

The planning and shaping of the volume is to a large extent the work of the directors of the research department, Dr. Hans Schönfeld and Mr. Nils Ehrenström. The editorial work and the preparation of the volumes for the press owes everything to the continuous labor of Miss Olive Wyon, who has also undertaken or revised the numerous translations, and in the final stages to the Rev. Edward S. Shillito, who during the last weeks accepted the responsibility of seeing the books through the press. Valuable help and advice was also given throughout the undertaking by Professor H. P. Van Dusen and Professor John Bennett of America.

J. H. OLDHAM
CHAIRMAN OF THE INTERNATIONAL
RESEARCH COMMISSION

LIST OF CONTRIBUTORS

WOOD, HERBERT GEORGE, M.A.

Director of Studies of Woodbrooke Settlement, Birmingham. Formerly Lecturer in History, Jesus College, Cambridge, and Lecturer on New Testament at Selly Oak Colleges.
Publications: Personal Economy and Social Reform; The Kingdom of God in the Teaching of Jesus; Rationalism and Historical Criticism; Venturers for the Kingdom (the Pilgrim Fathers); Living Issues in Religious Thought; Truth and Error of Communism; Christianity and the Nature of History; Communism: Marxist and Christian.

DODD, CHARLES HAROLD, M.A., HON.D.D., HON.S.T.D.

Norris-Hulse Professor of Divinity in the University of Cambridge. Formerly Lecturer in New Testament Greek and Exegesis, Mansfield College, Oxford; Rylands Professor of Biblical Criticism and Exegesis, University of Manchester; Speaker's Lecturer in Biblical Studies in the University of Oxford.
Publications: The Meaning of Paul for Today; The Gospel in the New Testament; The Authority of the Bible; The Epistle to the Romans; The Bible and the Greeks; The Parables of the Kingdom; The Apostolic Preaching.

BEVAN, EDWYN ROBERT, C.B.E., M.A., HON.D.LITT., HON.LL.D.

Fellow of New College, Oxford. Formerly Lecturer in Hellenistic History and Literature at King's College, London University.
Publications: Jerusalem under the High Priests; Indian Nationalism; Stoics and Sceptics; The Method in the Madness; The Land of Two Rivers; German Social Democracy during the War; Hellenism and Christianity; Later Greek Religion; Sibyls and Seers; Thoughts on Indian Discontents.

DAWSON, CHRISTOPHER, M.A.

Publications: Progress and Religion; Christianity and the New Age; Enquiries into Religion and Culture; The Modern Dilemma; The Spirit of the Oxford Movement; Mediaeval Religion; Religion and the Modern State.

LYMAN, EUGENE WILLIAM, M.A., D.D.

Marcellus Hartley Professor of Philosophy of Religion in Union Theological Seminary, New York. Formerly Professor of Philosophy of Religion and Christian Ethics, Oberlin School of Theology, Ohio.

Publications: Theology and Human Problems; Experience of God in Modern Life; The Meaning of Selfhood and Faith in Immortality; The Meaning and Truth of Religion. *With others,* Studies in Philosophy and Psychology; Religious Foundations; Religious Realism.

TILLICH, PAUL JOHANNES, D.PHIL., HON.D.THEOL.

Associate Professor of Philosophical Theology at Union Theological Seminary, New York. Formerly Professor extraordinarius at the University of Marburg; Professor ordinarius der Religionswissenschaft at the Technische Hochschule, Dresden; Professor honorarius of Theology at the University of Leipzig and Professor ordinarius of Philosophy at the University of Frankfurt a. Main.

Publications: Mystik und Schuldbewusstsein in Schellings philosophischer Entwicklung; Das System der Wissenschaften nach Gegenständen und Methoden; Die religiöse Lage der Gegenwart; Kairos, zur Geisterlage und Geisterwendung; Das Dämonische, ein Beitrag zur Sinndeutung der Geschichte; Kirche und Kultur; Religiöse Verwirklichung; Die sozialistische Entscheidung; The Interpretation of History.

WENDLAND, HEINZ-DIETRICH, DR.THEOL.

Professor of Theology at the University of Kiel. Formerly Dozent of Theology and Evangelical Studentenpfarrer at the University of Heidelberg.

Publications: Volk und Gott; Die Eschatologie des Reiches Gottes bei Jesus; Die Briefe an die Korinther; Das Staatsproblem in der evangelischen Theologie der Gegenwart; Die Mittler der paulinischen Botschaft; Der Herr der Zeiten; Die Kirche der Völker.

PIPER, OTTO, LIC.THEOL., HON.D.D.

Visiting Professor at Princeton Theological Seminary, U.S.A. Formerly Professor at Göttingen and Münster (Westphalia) and Lecturer in the University of Wales (Swansea and Bangor).

Publications: Das religiöse Erlebnis; Weltliches Christentum; Grundzüge der evangelischen Ethik; Gottes Wahrheit und die Wahrheit der Kirche; Recent Developments in German Protestantism.

TRANSLATORS

Professor Wendland's paper was translated by the Rev. E. L. Allen, and Professor Tillich's paper by Miss Olive Wyon.

THE KINGDOM OF GOD AND HISTORY

by

H. G. WOOD

THE KINGDOM OF GOD AND HISTORY

At the present time the question of the meaning of history is not only of theoretic interest but also of immediate practical importance. The war and the revolutions which accompanied or succeeded it appear to us like a great divide. Pre-war and post-war seem to stand for different worlds. We are oppressed with a *fin-de-siècle* consciousness. " The Decline of the West," " The End of an Era," " In the Shadow of Tomorrow " — such titles reflect a dominant reading of the signs of the times. Not so long ago authors were constantly using the expression " at the crossroads." Christianity, civilization, science, everything indeed was said to be at the crossroads. We know that we have to make momentous decisions, and on our decisions the future in large measure depends. Things will assuredly be different, but shall they be better or worse?

There is, then, a heightened sense of the importance of the events of our time. We live in a succession of crises, economic and political, and their full meaning only begins to dawn as the events recede into the past. We realize only too often that the failure of a nation or a government to act rightly or to act in time has brought disaster nearer and made genuine advance more difficult. The nations are apparently pursued by the nemesis of their past mistakes and sins, and sometimes we talk as if irresistible forces were hurrying us into inevitable war. It should be noted that such fatalism implies a view of history which requires examination and which must not readily be adopted by a Christian believer.

3

Our attitude towards the events of our time and our decisions as to personal action and public policy will certainly be affected by our interpretation of history. Political movements depend consciously or unconsciously on underlying conceptions of the nature of temporal happenings. In pre-war days both liberalism and socialism accepted an evolutionary philosophy and were guided by an optimistic belief in gradual progress. Today, the very idea of progress is called in question and to hanker after gradualism is to write one's self down a back number. Instead of the old belief in inevitable steady progress, moderns embrace a pathetic faith in the socially redemptive power of revolutionary violence. Lawless force is held to be the only possible midwife for the birth of a new social order. We have then the decisions of governments and the destinies of peoples determined by philosophies which interpret history in terms of irreconcilable class conflict or in terms of national and racial antagonism. Both these variants of the belief in war as the father of all things are accompanied by a secular messianic consciousness, adapted either to class or folk. The proletariat or the Aryan race is regarded as the creator of civilization and the bearer of salvation.

These conceptions of history, controlling for the moment the policies of large communities, have produced the present acute conflicts between the Christian church and the totalitarian states. What should be the relation of church, community and state in the modern world? A little while ago we might have assumed that the state is the servant of the community, that the state exists to protect the community and to further its social purposes. The church might also be regarded as the servant of the community, but her function is to educate the community to adopt social ideals and purposes in accord with God's will, and to persuade the community to live for the Kingdom of God. But now the state is the instrument in the hands of clear-sighted minorities resolved to discipline their respective communities to the acceptance of a particular creed and a particular secular end, whether it be the formation of a classless society or the revival of Roman imperialism or the realization of the Third German Reich. And the church of Christ is asked either to subordinate her message to these ends or to take the consequences.

How is the life and work of the church affected by the challenge of this situation? What is the task of the church at this turning point in history, and how is she to discharge it? Obviously the answer to these questions depends on the nature of the Kingdom of God, and on the relation of God's rule to temporal happenings. We have to ask ourselves and try to answer such questions as these: In what sense is the Kingdom of God present or future? Is the Kingdom actually present in some real measure, and is its presence realized only in the life of the church or is it embodied in forms of social and political life and in what are called cultural values? What is the relation of the Kingdom of God to history? Is it an ideal to be fully realized within history, an ideal social order to be established on earth at long last, or is the Kingdom essentially a way out of history, a super-historical reality? If the ultimate meaning of the Kingdom lies beyond history in a communion of saints triumphant and at rest in the enjoyment of that which is eternal, what is the relation between this realm of glory and the realm of grace here and now? How far are temporal happenings a manifestation of the Kingdom? Is there a progressive manifestation of the Kingdom in time, a history of redemption interwoven with world history? Is there such a thing as world history apart from the coming of the Kingdom? Is there such a thing as progress in civilization apart from the coming of the Kingdom? Can Christian faith discern in history an activity of God and discover God's providential overruling of events so that God's rule triumphs over and it may be through the very forces which oppose it?

The papers that follow are concerned with the answers to these and similar questions. The writers are drawn from three countries — America, England, Germany — and represent different confessions — Anglican, Catholic, Congregationalist, Lutheran. Readers will discover some essential agreements in the papers as well as noteworthy differences. Perhaps most important is the recognition of the distinctive character of history as the sphere of human responsibility. History is not the mere continuation of some natural process, and in consequence, it should be noted, history as a branch of knowledge can never take on the form of a natural science. Dr. Edwyn Bevan brings this out by endorsing Nicolai Hartmann's insistence on the distinction between purposive human action and the movements of inanimate nature. Professor Paul Tillich devotes a valuable section of his paper to the concept of history, emphasizing also the difference between mere becoming and history. He observes rightly that biological spontaneity may provide a transition from the mechanical changes of the natural order to the world of human purposive action, but ultimately biological spontaneity, life-movement, belongs to nature, not to history. This concept of history is still unfortunately too little appreciated, especially in Anglo-Saxon culture, but it is of vital importance for our understanding of the actual situation.

This concept of history, once grasped, raises many problems regarding the relation between nature and history, some of which are examined in Dr. Bevan's paper. History is manifestly conditioned by nature, but if human decisions count and if human responsibility is a reality, there can be no natural law of progress. From different angles of approach, both Professor Lyman and Mr. Christopher Dawson indicate the inadmissibility of any theory of natural or rational necessity in the story of human affairs. The former points out that " evolutionary optimistic philosophies of history, whether on a naturalistic or idealist basis, assuming a natural or rational law of development are obliged to derive the standards of progress by circular reasoning from the development process itself. Their adherents are left in a dilemma between a relativism which will justify each of our conflicting historical forces equally well, and a relapse from optimism to complete pessimism." Both the idealism of Hegel and the dialectical materialism of Karl Marx seem to issue in this moral relativism, which justifies whatever happens as a part of a necessary process. Christianity is committed to the view that the values for which men strive are not simply relative, and that conflicts are real, involving actual loss and gain. Mr. Dawson observes that " it is not only the materialistic interpretation of history but the idealistic interpretation as well which is irreconcilable with the traditional Christian view since it eliminates that sense of the divine otherness and transcendence, that sense of divine judgment and divine grace which are the very essence of the Christian attitude to history." Since values belong to this eternal and transcendent realm of God, history is not self-explanatory. History is shot through with superhistory, with the manifestation of the eternal in the midst of time.

Indeed apart from Christianity it is difficult to discover any meaning in history. It was Christianity which first gave men a sense of unity and purpose in history. This is well brought out in Dr. Wendland's paper. " Only from the Christian standpoint is there an actual universal history, a history of mankind, and not simply an entangled web of a thousand factors and tendencies, as well as not simply a juxtaposition of races and cultures which flourish and decay. History proceeds to and from Christ." Both Dr. Bevan and Mr. Dawson contrast with the Christian sense of purpose the dreary spectacle of endless repetition which changing human affairs presented to Marcus Aurelius. The Stoic was typical of that view of history as lacking permanent significance which may be found alike in Greek thought, in Hindu religious philosophy, and in Ecclesiastes. "Nothing new under the sun," and " vanity of vanities, all is vanity " sound the keynotes of a preacher, who proclaims not a Savior but the desperate need of a Savior. The spirit of romantic adventure was the child of Christian faith.

It may be questioned whether we ought to speak of " universal history " and whether the community of mankind is not potential rather than actual. For the Christian salvation itself has a history with its center in the incarnation of the Word in Christ. This for the Christian gives a final meaning to the tangled web of human experience; but may we not speak of a history of civilization, or perhaps better still histories of civilizations, as distinct from the story of man's redemption? This problem is handled at some length in a section of Professor Wendland's paper.

Two main conclusions stand out as essential to the Christian view of history. One is the element of conflict which is summed up in Augustine's idea of the City of God and its relation to world events and world forces. As Mr. Christopher Dawson puts it, there is the ever-renewed conflict between the community of charity and the community of self-will. This is not necessarily a conflict between church and state. It is waged within either institution and in the heart of every individual — faith and unfaith at grips with one another. But here in the modern world the conflict may be directly engaged between half-hearted and half-convinced Christians in organized bodies and states in the control of demonic forces, such as Professor Tillich discovers in capitalism, nationalism and bolshevism. It is characteristic of such forces that they include elements of good which the Christian church must acknowledge, and embody searching criticisms of the church which must be honestly faced. But the church has to bear witness to the unalterable character of fundamental moralities. It is sometimes said that the Christian church in the modern world must choose between communism and fascism. No such choice lies before us. We have to judge both communism and fascism, and indeed every form of government, in the light of God's commandments. The Christian objects to modern dictatorships not because they are dictatorships, nor yet because these dictatorships aim at the elevation of class or nation, but because they seek to gain their ends by disregarding the commandments: "Thou shalt do no murder; thou shalt not steal; thou shalt not bear false witness against thy neighbor." The church is bound to deny that the freedom of the workers or the honor of a nation can be maintained by lies and robbery and murder so prevalent in international relations today.

It may be that the political immoralism will end in the breakdown of civilization and the renewal of the Dark Ages. Indeed in a very real sense civilization has already broken down, and the nations have walked into the night. The conflict between those who believe that all is fair in the interests of class or nation and those who cling to some elementary decencies of human intercourse is acute and desperate, and the Christian church in such a conflict may be disowned and repudiated by political governments and driven out into the wilderness or to the catacombs. Professor Wendland, Professor Tillich and Mr. Dawson insist that the church may have to endure trial and persecution, is in fact exposed to trial and persecution already.

If less attention is paid to this side of the situation in the papers by Dr. Bevan and Professor Lyman, it may be due not only to the different positions of the church in America and Great Britain, but also to the second main conclusion which belongs to a Christian view of actual history. The faith and witness of the church have made a positive contribution to the historical life of Europe. The contribution is constantly ignored or discounted by rationalist critics and by impatient spiritual reformers, but it is none the less genuine. " That all political striving for power has to justify itself before a divine ruler of the world, that such striving finds its absolute limit in the idea of an eternal law set by God, and that the comity of European peoples, over and above all conflicting national interests, forms a community based on Christian morals, are all essentially medieval Christian thoughts." These thoughts may be repudiated by whole nations, but they live still and are undergoing a renascence alike in Catholic and Protestant Christianity.

In many directions, Christianity as a social gospel has been effective. We can discern the influence of Christianity in the idea of a world community, in the democratic movement, in the actual emancipation of the slaves, and in the development of the state in the service of brotherhood — a movement which can be traced back to public-spirited bishops like Synesius and his medieval successors and which now finds expression in the responsibility of the state for social services. Christianity has its own record of achievement and its own hope of progress.

There is a cumulative character about the social achievements and spiritual insights of the church *in via*. If the church experiences setbacks and apparent defeats, it must not abandon hope. It should be able and it will be able to make some positive constructive contribution to the creation of a new world civilization here and now to the comfort of man's distress and the confusion of false guides. May the prophet's word soon be forthcoming to establish the people's liberty!

THE KINGDOM OF GOD AND HISTORY

by

C. H. DODD

THE KINGDOM OF GOD AND HISTORY

CHRISTIANITY appeared in history as the heir of two traditions, the Hebrew and the Greek. It arose in a world in
which these two traditions had already met and mingled.
Hellenistic Judaism is a distinct and influential phenomenon of the period round about the beginning of the
Christian era, and its importance for the development of
early Christian thought was probably even greater than
it can be proved to be from the available direct evidence
of its influence. The central stream of Jewish thought,
which issued in the rabbinical Judaism of the Talmud,
appears to run in a separate channel, but there is reason
to believe that it was not always so exclusive of Gentile
elements as is commonly assumed. After all, Judaism had
undergone a long period of peaceful penetration by Hellenic influence before the ruthless attempt of the Seleucids
at *Gleichschaltung* provoked a reaction. There is evidence in the Talmud itself that Palestinian rabbis were at
least aware of Greek thought in its more popular and
widely diffused forms. On the other hand, Gentile thinkers in the Hellenistic world were often interested in the
religion of the Jews, and Judaism cannot be excluded from
the Oriental faiths which contributed to the development
of that movement of religious thought which is often described as " Hellenistic mysticism," or as " Gnosticism "
in the wider sense. The combination, therefore, of Jewish
and Greek elements in the thought of the New Testament
and other early Christian writings is not anything either
peculiar or unprecedented, nor is it often possible to say

with any certainty that *this* element was derived from
Jewish, *that* from Gentile sources. The pioneers of Christian theology made use of an idiom of thought which they
shared with other religious thinkers, both Jewish and
Gentile, in the Hellenistic world.

It is nevertheless possible to define in some measure
the distinctive character of the Jewish (or more properly
Hebrew) and of the Greek contribution to this amalgam.
We may best do so by referring to the problems which
most occupied the Greek mind, from the beginnings of
its adventures in philosophy — the problems of the One
and the Many, and of change or movement. The early
attempts to discover within the changing multiplicity of
the world of experience some unchanging and unifying
principle issued, after the somewhat naïve speculations
of the Ionian physicists, in the conviction that such a
principle could be found, if at all, only in the sphere of
thought or reason. It is rational thought that gives unity
to the manifold of experience, and while the data of the
senses are in perpetual flux, the rational meaning which
the mind discovers in them does not change, but, itself
remaining constant, is exemplified in their changes. To
this conviction Plato gave classical expression in his doctrine of Ideas, which, whether or not it was understood as
Plato intended it, supplied the main pattern of most philosophical thought of a religious kind in the Hellenistic
period. It was held that there were two orders of being —
the world of thought (κόσμος νοητός) and the world of the
senses (κόσμος αἰσθητός). The former consisted of a hierarchy of eternal Forms or Ideas, all summed up in the
unity of the Idea of Ideas. The Ideas correspond to the
universals of thought, but they exist independently of
the human mind, which, in rising from particulars as given
in sensible experience to the universals in which the mean-

ing of particulars resides, has communion with the κόσμος
νοητός.   Such communion alone is knowledge properly
so called.   For knowledge is of that which *is,* and of particulars it cannot be said that they *are,* but only that they
are in process of becoming and passing away (γένεσις καὶ
φθορά). That alone is fully real which is one and unchanging.   All that is manifold and changeable has in it an
element of not-being or unreality.

The other dominant philosophy of the time was Stoicism, which denied the independent or transcendent existence of the rational order, and discovered it as immanent
in the particulars of the sensible world.   But no less than
the Platonists, the Stoics assumed that the real is the rational.   The reality of the world is given not in the sensible (and individual) properties of things, but in the rational principle or meaning (λόγος) immanent in them,
apprehended and expressed in logical universals.   Stoicism, however, since the time of Posidonius in the first
century B.C., compromised or allied itself with Platonism,
and in the religious thought of the Hellenistic period the
Stoic doctrine of immanence is generally more or less
qualified in the direction of the Platonic doctrine of transcendence.   While in physics and in ethics the Stoic method
prevails, in metaphysics Hellenistic thought falls generally
into the dualistic mold of Platonism rather than into the
monistic mold of the older Stoicism.   It is a combination
of Platonism and Stoicism, but with Platonism as the ultimately dominant partner, that provided a *schema* for the
philosophy of religion in our period.

The type of religion which corresponded with this way
of thinking was one which offered salvation by a turning
away from this transient scene, and the contemplation of
eternal realities.   For such religion history could have no
proper significance.   For history is the sphere of the par-

ticular and the contingent, and therefore in this way of
thinking is irretrievably infected with unreality. God is
pure being ($\tau\grave{o}$ $\check{o}\nu\tau\omega s$ $\check{o}\nu$). To have communion with him
is, by definition, to escape from the sphere of the particular
and the contingent. History is movement, and God is the
Unmoved. History is change, and God is the Immutable.
History is in time and time is only " the moving image of
eternity," while God is essentially the Eternal. If the movement of history is to be brought into the scheme of a theistic universe at all, it must be believed to be movement
in a circle, which is the only perfect kind of movement,
since it is movement about a fixed point, and fulfills its
course in returning perpetually to its beginning. The
cyclic theory of history was adumbrated in Platonism, and
made into a dogma by the Stoics, who postulated an endless series of cycles of time, each ending with a general
conflagration, and beginning afresh with a " rebirth "
($\pi\alpha\lambda\iota\gamma\gamma\epsilon\nu\epsilon\sigma\acute{\iota}\alpha$). Whatever happens has already happened
innumerable times before, and will happen innumerable
times again. By this device the apparent particularity and
contingency of history is overcome, for the apparently
particular is subsumed under a constant law of recurrence.
This law is the destiny ($\epsilon\grave{\iota}\mu\alpha\rho\mu\acute{\epsilon}\nu\eta$), or necessity ($\grave{\alpha}\nu\acute{\alpha}\gamma\kappa\eta$),
by which the whole phenomenal universe is determined.
Religion offered an escape from $\epsilon\grave{\iota}\mu\alpha\rho\mu\acute{\epsilon}\nu\eta$, by showing
how the soul could ascend out of the $\kappa\acute{o}\sigma\mu os$ $\alpha\grave{\iota}\sigma\theta\eta\tau\acute{o}s$ in a
" flight to pure being " ($\kappa\alpha\tau\alpha\phi\upsilon\gamma\grave{\eta}$ $\pi\rho\grave{o}s$ $\tau\grave{o}$ $\check{o}\nu$).

For the Hebrews, on the other hand, movement in time,
that is to say history, is the field of reality, and God is the
living God whose mighty acts make history. The difference is well illustrated by the interpretation of the divine
name YHWH given in the Hebrew text and in the Sep-
tuagint respectively of the classical passage Exodus 3:14.
In Hebrew it is explained by the words אהיה אשר אהיה. In

Greek it is represented by the participial phrase ὁ ὤν. This is a timeless present implying existence as such. We might render it " the Self-existent." It is a designation of deity congenial to the Greek mind, though the fact that even Philo the Jew often turns it into the neuter τὸ ὄν betrays a characteristic Greek uneasiness about ascribing personality to the Absolute. The Hebrew אהיה, however, does not mean " I am." Whether we translate it " I am wont to be " or " I will be " — either is an approximation to the meaning of this form of the verb — its implications are not static but dynamic. It designates God as him who is known in his activity in the continuous or successive processes of history. As the Hebrew is aware of himself as living and acting in time, so he conceives God as living and acting in time, though God, unlike man, has all the time he needs. He thinks of God as fully personal, in terms of will and purpose rather than of essence. The will of God is known in his Law, his purpose is discerned in his mighty acts in history. Such knowledge is sufficient for man. It is not inability to know God in his essence that marks man's separation from him, but alienation from his will, which is sin. Hebrew religious thought arrived at monotheism not through a conception of abstract unity, but through the idea of the Kingdom of God as the effective reign of a righteous and universal will.[1]

The Hebrew mind (until it came under Greek influence) was not interested in the metaphysical puzzles of the one and the many, identity and change, being and becoming. Its problem was a moral one. How could the facts of evil in human experience be reconciled with the uni-

---

[1] Much of this paragraph, with a sentence or two in the context, is reproduced from my lecture on " Christianity and Hellenism," in the Harvard Tercentenary Publications (Harvard University Press, 1937). I am grateful to the holders of the copyright for permission to use the material here.

versal reign of a righteous God? Its answer was given, not in philosophy, but in eschatology. Eschatology, as it emerges in the prophets and apocalyptists, is an attempt to give a satisfying account of the ways of God in terms of the time process, assumed to be real, and the proper field of the divine action. The world was conceived as started on its course by the divine fiat. Into this world evil entered, in some way which was never very clearly defined, but in any case in a way which did not impugn the sovereignty of the one righteous God. The subsequent course of history is divinely directed to an end in which evil will be finally eliminated, and the will of God will be manifestly, as it has always been really, supreme: " His kingdom shall appear throughout all his creation." History is thus not a series of cyclic movements returning upon themselves, but a real succession of particular, concrete, unrepeatable events in which the prophetic eye can discern stages in the working out of the divine purpose. God called Abraham from Ur; he brought up Israel out of the land of Egypt; he gave the Law at Sinai; he drove out the heathen from his inherit-ance; he raised up David to be king; he punished his people by the rod of Assyria and Babylon; he redeemed them by the hand of Cyrus the Persian. In form this is the history of a single people, but in intention it is universal history. If the Lord brought up Israel out of Egypt, he also brought the Philistines from Caphtor and the Syrians from Kir, and he has designs for Assyria and Egypt as well as for the chosen race. But the essential concreteness and particu-larity of history are expressed in the (instinctive and in-evitable) selection of a series of events experienced in their particularity by the community to which they are specially relevant. When Philo treats the story of the call of Abra-ham as a universally applicable symbol of the turning of the soul from the things of sense to the quest of reality, he is

abandoning the characteristically Hebrew valuation of concrete history. What the Old Testament affirms is that at a
particular time, a particular individual, Abraham,[2] was
called to leave a particular place, Ur of the Chaldees, and
that this event led to concrete consequences in history.
Any attempt to qualify or eliminate the particularity of
history is contrary to the genius of Hebrew religious
thought. In things that happen, it sees the hand of God,
and to happen means to have a particular and non-inter-
changeable *locus* in time and space.

Admittedly, in any such particular event the divine purpose is not completely expressed; for purpose implies a
process working towards an end, and until the end is attained the purpose remains unfulfilled. Thus the prophetic view of God's dealings, as it looks back to creation,
also looks forward to the consummation, the Day of the
Lord. What primitive mythology lies behind that concept
we cannot say. In the hands of the prophets and their successors it becomes a symbol for the expected summing-up of
the historical process, in which the purpose of God in history, divined only by faith at present, will be completely
revealed and fulfilled. In much prophetic thought the Day
of the Lord, whatever miracles may attend its coming, and
however conclusive and universal its effects, remains in a
real sense an event within history, particular and concrete
like all other events. It will bring a restoration of the kingdom of David, a great and final victory of Israel over its
enemies, a concourse of Gentiles to the Temple on Mount
Zion, an assembly of nations in the Valley of Jehoshaphat,
or the like. But with the rise of apocalyptic there is a

[2] If, as some critics hold, Abraham is the name of a clan, or even of the
deity worshiped by the clan, it still remains true that at some point in history the sense of a divine " call " to the clan arose, and arose, surely,
through some individual leader, even if the date to be assigned to the event
be later than that traditionally assigned to Abraham.

change.   There will be a new heaven and a new earth, the
dead will rise, the living will be transfigured into forms of
glory, the righteous will enter into immortal life with the
angels.   In other words, the End is no longer an event in
history.   It lies beyond this order of time and space.   How
far these apocalyptic ideas were affected by contact with
Persian or other foreign ways of thought, it is difficult to
say; but the development is nevertheless in one sense at
least a fulfilment of ideas already implied in the prophetic
eschatology.   This needs some further explanation.

When we say that the Hebrews experienced the divine in
history, we must beware of suggesting that they thought of
history as divine in its own right, a self-determining process
holding its meaning within itself.   The object of the prophetic faith is no merely immanent divinity.   The purpose
manifest in history is the purpose of a transcendent God,
who though he is revealed in history is by no means confined within time and space.   The meaning of history,
therefore, is determined by that which lies beyond history.
The events in which the divine action is recognized are
interpreted as *interventions* of God from his throne on
high.   Consequently the End, even when it is thought of as
the last event in history, will have the character of a final
irruption of the supra-historical into history.   When, therefore, the apocalyptists describe it in terms appropriate to
no conceivable event in history, they effectively indicate
the transcendent character which must belong to it.   In
reaching its conclusion, history passes beyond itself.

The prophetic and apocalyptic eschatology, then, provides a *schema* within which the movement of history, in
its concrete particularity, may be accepted as the revelation
of God, with the proviso that that which has not yet happened must be postulated as the necessary fulfilment without which the revelation remains incomplete.   In this sense

Judaism is an historical religion. It is such in distinction
from nature-religion and from mysticism. In mysticism
man turns away from the world of things and events to the
eternal and unchanging world of the spirit. Nature-
religion finds the divine in the world of things and events,
but in those aspects of it which are recurrent, and may be
regarded as exemplifications of unchanging laws, and not
in the particular and non-recurrent events which make up
history. Among the Greeks, primitive nature cults gave
rise to mystery religions, and were taken up into the higher
paganism of the Hellenistic period. The Hebrew prophets, on the other hand, in their conflict with the fertility
cults of the Baalim, decisively repudiated all such worship.
The ground for this is clear. Nature is in itself non-moral
as it is non-personal. History is the sphere in which character counts and moral issues are involved. It is, therefore,
the proper sphere for the revelation of a God who is personal and cares for righteousness. Only after God has been
recognized in the moral and personal order of history can
the subpersonal order of nature become also a safe medium
for religious experience.

Considered as a theistic interpretation of history, Jewish
eschatology labors under a serious defect. The prophets
interpret particular events as acts of God, but in order that
this interpretation may be valid, the particular event must
be regarded in the light of an event which has not yet happened — the coming of the Day of the Lord — and this
event is not matter of experience, but of a faith which
clothes itself in fantasy. Thus the prophecies of the second
Isaiah interpret the return of Jewish exiles under the decree of Cyrus as the redemption of God's people, but they
associate with it ideal or fantastic features which have no
correspondence with what actually happened. The post-
exilic prophets associate messianic ideas with the rebuilding

of the Temple, but they have to reassure the people, who are depressed by the insignificance of the new building, by affirming that the Lord will suddenly come to his Temple and fill it with glory. This appeal to the future to verify the prophetic interpretation of the present runs all through the Old Testament. The logic of Jewish eschatology might be stated thus: The exodus from Egypt (with all the mighty acts that followed) was an act of God, the Creator of the universe, since by it he made a people for himself, a people of kings and priests, his Son, his Anointed. But the facts of history seem to deny this, since the people of God forsakes him for idols, and goes into captivity. Its actual status in history is not apparently that willed by God. This denial, however, will be turned into affirmation when in the future God acts finally and reveals the people of the saints of the Most High in the glory of the age to come. The whole meaning of history will then be clear. At present it is given only to seers and prophets, with whom is the secret of the Lord. The End, as revealed to them in vision, or by the Word of the Lord, is for them absolutely certain, so certain that it always seems all but here. Nevertheless it is to vision and not to facts of experience that they appeal for the interpretation of contemporary history. The vision is indeed a vision of an event, an event for them as real and actual as any event of the past or the present, but it can after all be described only in fantastic or mythological terms, since it belongs to the unrealized future.

The prophetic interpretation of history thus includes what we may call a tension between the ideal and the actual. But these are terms which belong rather to our Greek heritage of thought than to the Hebrew thought which we are now attempting to set forth. The Hebrew mind (until it comes under foreign influence) does not think in terms of an ideal world imperfectly actualized in the world of our experience. That which exists eternally is nothing but the will or purpose of the transcendent and personal God, and that will is expressed in a process in time, completely expressed only when the process is complete. In the apocalyptists, however, who carry on the prophetic tradition, there is an approximation to the Greek view, in that we have the conception of a heavenly order eternally existing, and accessible in vision to the seer, which in the end will invade and transform the historical order. The age to come is not simply another period of history, lying as yet in the future, but an order of being essentially superior to the present order, which will enter into human experience when this order ends. It still remains, however, that salvation for man does not consist in turning away from the historical order and entering here and now into the eternal and ideal world. He must wait in expectancy for the final act of God by which the historical process will be wound up, and the life of the age to come laid open to those whom he has chosen.

Primitive Christianity took over the *schema* of Jewish eschatology. Like Judaism it regarded history as the sphere of the divine action which is the revelation of a transcendent and personal God. Like Judaism it rejected all ideals of recurrent cycles in history; it looked back to a real beginning and forward to a real end, and conceived the process from beginning to end as directed by the purpose of God. But it made one profound and fundamental change. Whereas Jewish eschatology looked to the close of the historical process as the necessary fulfilment upon which the meaning of history depends, Christianity found the fulfilment of history in an actual series of events within history — namely the life, death and resurrection of Jesus Christ, and the emergence of the church as the bearer of his Spirit. History, indeed, still goes on, and at long last it will have an ending. But meanwhile, the true *eschaton*, the event in which its meaning is conclusively revealed, has become an object of experience. This conviction is expressed in the fundamental thesis of early Christian preaching, that prophecy is fulfilled in the coming of Christ. It is true that much of the mythological apparatus of apocalyptic is retained to describe his expected second coming at the end of history. But its character is altered when the end of the world is thought of as the return of a Lord who has already come. It is one thing to believe that at long last the Lord will come, and to have recourse to pure fantasy for a picture of his coming; it is another thing to believe that the Lord has come, and that whatever may be the final issue of history, it can do no more than unfold the meaning already given in his historical coming. Hope of the unknown takes form and character from that which is already known. The understanding of history, and of God's action in history, no longer depends upon " vision " of an imaginary future. On the contrary, the Christian vision of the future depends upon experience of actual historical events. Moreover, while an outlook upon the end of the world remains a part of the Christian gospel, its central purport is the proclamation that in the coming of Christ we have the conclusive entrance of God into history, which prophecy and apocalypse had associated with the End. While parts of the eschatological tradition are still given a future application, Christian writers ransack the Old Testament to accumulate evidence that all that the prophets had said of the final issue of the divine purpose was fulfilled in Christ. Language which had been used to describe the Day of the Lord, or the age to come, they consciously, deliberately, and consistently apply to the facts of history as experienced by the church. Whatever may be said of the second advent of the Lord, the sense of the preparatory, the provisional, the incomplete, which is an inseparable element in all Old Testament prophecy, has no place in the New Testament. The Lord has come.

The effect of this is to disrupt the scheme of Jewish eschatology. Formally, indeed, the Christian gospel keeps very closely to that scheme. As for the prophets, so for the New Testament writers, the revelation of God is given in a series of concrete historical events, and the *eschaton,* in which the series culminates, has the same concrete and particular character, for it consists in a unique historical episode " under Pontius Pilate." As for the apocalyptists, so for early Christianity, the *eschaton* is the breaking-in of a supra-historical order (a " new creation "). But the underlying assumptions of Jewish eschatology are profoundly modified. The prophetic and apocalyptic interpretation of history assumed that the working out of the divine purpose to a climax would fill up the whole period of history (" this age "), and history would end with its fulfilment. The gospel declares that within history an event happened in which the whole purpose of God is fulfilled. That which is beyond history has entered into history, and yet history goes on. It is clear that a simple time-scheme such as that of the older eschatology can no longer suffice. There is in history something other than movement in time towards a goal which will be the end of history.

Attempts to reconstruct eschatology so as to allow for the new facts while yet retaining the traditional scheme (such as those which we find in Mark 13, 2 Thessalonians, and the Revelation of John) ultimately broke down. Millenarianism was dropped or fell into the background in the main church tradition. The founders of Christian theology sought more appropriate ways of expressing the realized eschatology which lies at the heart of the gospel. In doing so they had recourse to Greek forms of thought. The

doctrine of the two orders of being was used to interpret
the paradoxical situation in which the church found itself,
at the overlapping point, so to speak, of two ages.   The
Christian lived " in the flesh," that is to say within the conditions of space, time and matter by which history is
bounded.   Yet he had experienced a " new creation," he
had " tasted the powers of the Age to Come," he had been
" born again " out of the sphere of flesh into that of spirit,
had died to the world and risen again with Christ, and now
lived with him " in the heavenly places."   There is here
something analogous to the Greek conception of an ascent
of the soul out of the phenomenal sphere into communion
with the κόσμος νοητός.   Already in Paul we find language
which recalls that of " Hellenistic mysticism."   In the
Epistle to the Hebrews the doctrine of the two orders, the
real world and the world of shadows, lies alongside the eschatological doctrine of the two ages.   In the Fourth Gospel the eschatological *schema* has been transformed almost
out of recognition, and the idea of eternal life through the
knowledge of God is presented in terms which closely re-
semble those of Hellenistic religious thought, especially as
it is expressed in Philo and the Hermetic writings.

It would, however, be a misunderstanding to suppose
that in using such language the New Testament writers intend to abandon the reality of history, or to offer salvation
by a world-denying " flight to pure being."   Paul's so-called
" Christ-mysticism," for example, cannot be treated as a
mere variant of " Hellenistic mysticism."   Its key-phrase,
" in Christ," has reference to the concept of the " body "
of Christ, whose " members " are baptized " into Christ."
The expression σῶμα Χριστοῦ is a theological description
of a concrete historical phenomenon, the Christian church.
Paul begins the history of the church with the call of Abraham, to whom the promise was given: " In thee shall all

nations be blessed." There was thus called into being, in the purpose of God, a universal society, the people of God. That purpose is a "selective purpose" (κατ' ἐκλογὴν πρόθεσις). Its first act is the selection of Abraham out of the body of mankind "in Adam." It is manifested in an historical process of selection among the descendants of Abraham. Isaac is called, not Ishmael; Jacob, not Esau. Out of Israel a faithful remnant is chosen, to represent the true Israel of God. But while Israel remains in bondage to the Law, the true Israel, which is God's son, cannot come into actual or effective existence. For through the Law, sin, which obstructs the revelation of the sons of God, is increased. So it comes about that the "seed" of Abraham, to which the promise applies, is finally concentrated in a single individual, God's only Son, in whom all prophecy, which declared the purpose of God, is fulfilled.

This must suffice as a brief summary of what is a brilliant and highly original reinterpretation of Old Testament history, giving to the prophetic interpretation a unity, clarity, and consistency which it could not possess until the fulfilment entered into history and became object of experience. But while all this is history, it has a supra-historical aspect. Christ is on the one hand the Seed of Abraham, the heir of an historical tradition; he is on the other hand the man from heaven, the divine image, the power and the wisdom of God, through whom all things were made. The emergence of the church which is his Body is not only the final phase of the history of Israel, but also the sphere of the "new creation" and within that sphere men are "blessed with every spiritual blessing in the heavenly places." The unity of Jew and Gentile in the church is the pledge in experience of the promised unity of mankind, indeed of all things in heaven and earth, destined to be "summed up in Christ." At the same time the church itself has a history.

It grows as a body, or is built up as a temple. The unity of mankind given in the universality of Christ is progressively to be realized through the comprehension of individuals of every race, and perfected through the exercise of the χαρίσματα of the Spirit granted to them, above all through the supreme χάρισμα of ἀγάπη. There will be an End when the church, or redeemed humanity, has grown into the stature of the fullness of Christ. But there will be nothing in the End which is not already given implicitly to the church.[3] Christ has already conquered the powers of evil, and in him men already have access to the glorious and immortal life of the eternal order.

In the Epistle to the Hebrews the doctrine of the two orders of being and that of the two ages lie side by side. Fundamentally the author's outlook is Platonic, in the same sense as Philo's. The κόσμος νοητός, God's eternal temple in " the heaven itself," is the only true reality. The phenomenal order is a play of shadows. The Jewish religion (and any other religion on the same level) operates with shadows, and not with realities. The author has not Paul's robust Hebrew sense of history. He does not see the Old Testament as the record of a process in which God's purpose is working towards its fulfilment. It is all through no more than a symbol of that which is perpetually existent " within the veil," which the saints of the old dispensation divined by "faith " (ἀφανοῦς ὑπόληψις, as Philo called it). But in the Christian dispensation there is a " way through

---

[3] The most striking statement of this is in 1 Cor. 2:9 sqq. The final issue of the divine purpose is " that which eye hath not seen nor ear heard, neither hath it entered into the heart of man " — it is the " wholly other " — and yet this is already revealed to the church through the Spirit. Elsewhere the idea is expressed in the doctrine of the ἀρραβών or ἀπαρχή, which means (to put it somewhat crudely) that the ultimate blessedness is qualitatively or intensively identical with the present experience of the church, but quantitatively or extensively greater.

the veil," and Christians have access " to Mount Sion, to an innumerable company of angels, to the spirits of just men made perfect, to God the judge of all," that is to say, to the κόσμος νοητός where God is eternally praised by his " powers " (cf. *Corpus Hermeticum* 1. 26). So far this looks like a typically Hellenistic doctrine of salvation, in which Christianity has the character of a superior form of *gnosis*. But this is not the author's intention. For access to the eternal order, within the veil, is not a matter of initiation into " knowledge of the supramundane "; [4] it is the consequence of an historical act, Christ's self-dedication to death in fulfilment of the will of God. His death is at once a part of history, the result on the one side of his obedience learned through suffering, on the other side of the " opposition of sinners," and also an eternal and perfectly real sacrifice in the heavenly temple, of which all sacrifices in the phenomenal order are mere shadows. It is clear that we have here a distinctive conception of history. It is neither real in its own right, so to speak, nor is it altogether the shadowy symbol of eternal reality. At one point it is completely real, because in it the eternal reality is completely expressed. The system of Jewish religious ordinances, here taken as the relevant portion of the phenomenal order, is not only the symbol of the eternal " Idea " of sacrifice and priesthood, but also an anticipatory type of the historical sacrifice of Christ, which thus has, in relation to the rest of history, the same kind of value as the κόσμος νοητός itself. As for the future, the author retains the belief that the phenomenal order, " the things that are shaken," will pass away, leaving intact the " kingdom which cannot be shaken," which Christians have already " received." While, therefore, the Epistle to the Hebrews is

---

[4] Εὐαγγέλιόν ἐστι κατ' αὐτοὺς (scil. τοὺς βασιλιδιανούς) ἡ τῶν ὑπερκοσμίων γνῶσις (Hippolytus, *Philosophumena* vii. 27.7).

more definitely " Hellenistic " than Paul, it holds to the fundamental Jewish conviction that history is the field of the divine action, and to the primitive Christian conviction that such action is conclusive in the historical episode of the life and death of Christ.

In the Fourth Gospel this conclusiveness is most clearly and consistently affirmed. The Prologue is a concise and masterly statement of the relation of the coming of Christ to the whole temporal order. The " Logos " of which it speaks may be taken, in accordance with the usage of the term in Hellenistic writers, to stand for the rational principle or meaning immanent in the universe, conceived however both platonically as a world of real existences (ἀληθινά), and, still more emphatically, in Jewish fashion as the " Word " of the transcendent God. This Logos pervades the whole world as life, and is immanent in man as light (the light of reason). But it is never thought of as merely immanent, for as the Word of God it invades this world from the eternal order, as in Hebrew history the Word of the Lord " came to his own," to be received by some, rejected by others. Finally, in the coming of Christ, the Logos was made flesh. The implication is that the Logos in creation, that is, the divine meaning of nature, and the Logos in history, that is, the divine meaning of history, is revealed in the historical episode narrated in the subsequent chapters of the Gospel, and only there fully and conclusively revealed. Ὁ λόγος σὰρξ ἐγένετο: no more final relation of the eternal to the temporal order can be conceived. There is therefore no place for a " second coming " in the sense of popular Christian eschatology. It still remains for the " flock " of Christ to be completed, for all the children of God to be brought into one, including those who are now in their tombs, and in this sense the Gospel includes an outlook upon the future. But the knowledge of God which is eternal life in no sense depends upon that which is yet to happen. " The hour is coming *and now is* " — that is the characteristic formula of this author. Already the harvest of the world is ripe. God is worshiped here and now in the spiritual temple, now is the judgment of this world, now is the prince of this world cast out, and he who believes already possesses eternal life. Thus the episode of the life, death and resurrection of Jesus is history, but it is *Endgeschichte,* eschatological history, history with its full meaning revealed. While the idea of salvation expounded in the Fourth Gospel is framed very largely in Hellenistic terms, it is always essentially related to history, and never passes over into a world-denying mysticism such as that of Philo or the Hermetic writers, with whom, in many respects, this evangelist has much affinity. Knowledge of God, union with God, rebirth into eternal life, are attained not by an individual initiation into *gnosis,* but by participation in the community of the " friends " of Christ. In this community his Spirit dwells as Paraclete, in consequence of his exaltation or ascent to the Father, which was accomplished by his sufferings and death under Pontius Pilate.

The theologians of the New Testament, then, make greater or less use of the categories of Hellenistic thought, to express the absoluteness of the revelation in Christ, but none of them leaves the ground of the Hebraic faith that God acts in history, and that the meaning of history is revealed in the coming of his Kingdom. That element in the Hebraic view which they leave behind is the assumption that for this revelation, in any full way, we must wait until history ends. The *eschaton* is for them no longer the last term in a temporal series, but the qualitatively final or ultimate, entering into the midst of history in a decisive crisis by which the meaning of the whole is determined.

While, therefore, the gospel is continuous with the prophetic religion of the Old Testament, it involves a profound and indeed shattering modification of the prophetic
view of history.   If we now ask, what led to this modification, the answer clearly is that it was made necessary by
events that actually happened, and challenged interpretation.   But if we further ask, who was responsible for this
interpretation, the answer is not so clear.   Behind Paul,
and the author to the Hebrews, and the Fourth Evangelist,
lies a common conviction, to which these thinkers give
varied theoretical expression, but which none of them is
likely to have originated.   It is something assumed in the
whole New Testament.   If now we look back to the presentation of the teaching of Jesus in the Synoptic Gospels,
it seems natural to conclude that, if this presentation can
be trusted to give anything like a true impression, it was
Jesus himself who first interpreted his own ministry, death,
and resurrection as the breaking-in of the Kingdom of God.
The teaching has a paradoxical character, sometimes suggesting that the Kingdom of God is yet to come and sometimes that it is already here.   A formula, in fact, like that
of the Fourth Gospel — " the hour cometh and now is " —
would aptly fit what is said of the Kingdom of God in the
Synoptic Gospels.   But while there are pronouncements
cast into the form of prediction, it seems clear that the main
purport of the whole is that the eschatological hope is now
fulfilled.   " Today is this Scripture fulfilled in your ears ";
" Blessed are your eyes, for they see; for many prophets and
kings desired to see the things ye see and saw them not."
The harvest of the world is ripe and awaits the laborers.
The sin of man, from the murder of Abel onwards, is visited
on " this generation."   On the other hand the messianic
banquet is spread for those who accept the invitation:
" Come for all things are now ready."   In the authority

with which Jesus speaks, and the power with which he acts, the Kingdom of God is revealed: " If I by the finger of God cast out demons, then the Kingdom of God is come upon you." That Jesus goes to his death as " King of the Jews," predicting his resurrection as " Son of Man," is in harmony with the implication of his teaching that the Kingdom of God has come with the coming of the Messiah.

The simplest hypothesis seems to be that the common conviction which underlies the Pauline Epistles, the Epistle to the Hebrews and the Fourth Gospel, and indeed the whole New Testament, was based upon the teaching of Jesus about the Kingdom of God,[5] understood in the light of his death and resurrection. It is only clarified and in a measure rationalized by being translated into terms of an eschatology modified by the use of Greek categories, without these categories ever being allowed to obscure the fundamental valuation of history which underlies all eschatology.

The Christian view of history, then, is one which refuses to identify it simply with the time-process. It is not to be considered as a development in time towards a goal yet unknown. The story of Israel in the Old Testament can readily be interpreted, and up to a point truly interpreted, as an " evolution of religion." But if it is so considered, the product of that evolution is not Christ or Christianity, but the Judaism which destroyed Jesus, to its own cost. As Paul acutely pointed out, the history of Israel has a paradoxical character, in that it proceeds from a divine purpose, yet that purpose is apparently frustrated, as the field within which it works, that of the people of God, is progressively narrowed, until at last it is represented by one single individual, who is destroyed by the very institutions through

---

[5] For a fuller treatment, I may be allowed to refer to my book *The Parables of the Kingdom.*

which Israel had kept and developed its identity. In Christ the people of God dies, is crucified to the world. But in Christ the people of God rises from the dead and enters upon newness of life. Not development in time, but death and resurrection, judgment and a new creation, is the character of the history — the *Endgeschichte* — in which the purpose of God is brought to fulfilment. The series of events which makes up the history of Israel served to bring about a situation (" the fullness of time ") in which the Kingdom of God came upon men. It came as judgment and as redemption, as gift and as challenge. It came as the " wholly other " which yet gives meaning to this world.

In other words, history was at that point re-created from an inner center in which " the powers of the age to come," or of the eternal world, were in action. It was determined, not by the horizontal forces of development within time, but by the vertical impact of forces from the unseen. In the light of this fact we see that the essential meaning of history is always of this kind. The development of events in time, determined by natural and economic causes, and by the conflict of human ideals, is not in itself the process that brings the Kingdom of God. It provides successive situations in which the powers of the Kingdom reveal themselves. The response of men to the challenge of such a situation helps to determine a further situation, in which the challenge is delivered afresh. So far as progress can be affirmed, it consists in the enlargement of the area of facts which are faced by men in their response to the challenge of the Kingdom of God, as for example the conflict to which the church is called today, in Europe, Asia and America, covers a wider field of human life in all respects than that of the first century — not merely geographically wider, but wider in the sense of including a whole range of aspects of human life of which the first Christians could be but feebly aware, such as those of economics and of the scientific control of nature. But this is by no means to say that we have progressed towards the realization of a utopian " Kingdom of God " upon earth. The expansion and enrichment of civilization, in which progress is most easily recognized, brings with it not only much that is clearly good, but also new and more powerful forms of evil, and in conflict with such evil the powers of the Kingdom of God are manifested afresh.

The Kingdom of God is not something yet to come. It came with Jesus Christ, and in its coming was perceived to be eternal in its quality. That eternal quality is manifested in time by the continuous life of the church, centered in the sacrament in which the crisis of the death and resurrection of Christ is perpetually made present. In this sacrament it celebrates the coming of the Lord, which is at once his historical coming in humiliation, and his coming in the glory of the Father with the holy angels. " The hour cometh and now is," when we behold the Kingdom of God come with power. It comes with judgment upon the evil of the world, and the church always knows that " it is time for judgment to begin from the House of God." We stand before the judgment-seat of Christ, and there we know that the judgment of God is also forgiveness, and that through death we rise to life. It is through this process of judgment and redemption, death and resurrection, that history is always re-created from an inner center, that is, out of the experience of those who have " received the Kingdom of God," and are thereby committed to the labor and conflict through which the Kingdom is revealed.

When we pray " Thy Kingdom come," we are not praying that at long last history may end with utopia or the millennium, but that in *this* situation in which we stand the reign of God may be made manifest after the pattern of its

revelation in Christ (through " the fellowship of his sufferings and the power of his resurrection "). The future,
which can bring with it nothing to supersede that revelation of the Kingdom of God, is not our concern, nor is it in
the future that we must seek the perfection of which the
temporal order is not capable, but in that other world in
which the ultimate meaning of history resides, where " our
life is hid with Christ in God."

THE KINGDOM OF GOD AND HISTORY

by

EDWYN BEVAN

THE KINGDOM OF GOD AND HISTORY

THE term " Kingdom of God " sounds as if it proclaimed in the first place the sovereignty of God's will, but, strange as it may seem, one of the things to which the term immediately calls attention is the fact that in an important part of the universe, a part spiritually important, though materially insignificant, the will of God is *not* done. If everything which took place in the universe was a sovereign act of God, if the act of every finite will was performed in absolute accordance with God's will, everything in the universe would be Kingdom of God, and there would be no point in speaking of the Kingdom as something distinctive. The Kingdom of God is a significant term only because of the implied contrast with a Kingdom of Evil, a sphere in which finite beings act in opposition to God, or in disregard of God. How it is possible, if God is almighty, for things to be brought about by any finite will displeasing to God is, of course, one of the hardest problems in any Christian philosophy of religion. Yet that God's will is *not* at present done on earth as it is in heaven is presupposed in the most familiar and most authoritatively sanctioned of prayers.

Christians generally hold that in all processes of subhuman nature, except in so far as they are interfered with by wrong choices on the part of spiritual beings, human or daemonic, God's will is perfectly done; it is only a spiritual being, endowed with the power of choice, who could possibly go against God's will. This much at any rate seems to any logical thought essentially involved in the idea of omnipotence. If any being can oppose God, that can only be because God in some mysterious way restricts, in regard to such a being, his own power, because he wills to allow his will to be opposed.

But supposing any process of sub-human nature could thwart the divine will, there would seem no way of regarding that as other than a failure, a coming short, of God's power: God could not then be omnipotent. If then none of the myriad luminous material masses we see distributed through space has any spiritual beings inhabiting it, such as this earth has, then all the wheeling systems of the universe, moved only by the laws applying to inanimate matter, perfectly carry out God's plan. It is only on this almost infinitesimal speck in space that so astounding a thing takes place — God's will opposed, not done. To the ancient Greeks the eternal regularity of the starry skies seemed the pure manifestation of beauty and order in contrast with the manifold confusions and lawlessness of earth, and a Greek might have prayed that petition of the Lord's Prayer, meaning by the heaven in which God's will was done, not any invisible spiritual world, but the literal material heavens. George Meredith has expressed the same idea. He pictures Satan flying by night over the earth with its sad population of sinners.

> Soaring through wider zones that pricked his scars
> With memory of the old revolt from Awe,
> He reached a middle height, and at the stars,
> Which are the brain of heaven, he looked, and sank.
> Around the ancient track marched, rank on rank,
> The Army of unalterable law.
>
> (*Lucifer in Starlight*)

Of course, in so far as the movement of the heavenly bodies is the movement of mere inanimate masses of matter according to unvarying laws, they do not offer any real

contrast to the lawlessness of spiritual beings. The only
contrast to that can be the voluntary obedience of spiritual
beings, and Jesus certainly did not mean the literal skies
by the heaven in which God's will is done. He meant
an unseen world of spiritual beings who by their own
choice yielded themselves perfectly to accomplish what
God willed.

Yet the perfect carrying out of the divine plan by the
processes of sub-human nature, although something altogether different from the voluntary obedience of a spiritual being, is an important factor of the problem when
we come to consider the Kingdom of God and history.
For history is made in part by the voluntary choices of men
and in part by natural processes in which, except in so far
as they are interfered with by human volition, God's will
must be perfectly carried out. History is the total sequence
of human lives on this planet with their experiences and
their voluntary choices; the situation which each of us
finds, when he comes as an individual into the world, is
due to the innumerable voluntary choices made by men
and women in the past, and we, by our voluntary choices,
each in our own measure, determine what the next moment in history is to be. The future will be different
according to what men decide now.

Yet this long concatenation of events and experiences is
made only in part by human wills. The choices do not
take place in a vacuum, but in a material and animal environment which suggests them, which impinges at every
point upon the life of men and largely determines how far
the event actually corresponds with what was desired when
the choice was made. Yet further than that, each act of
choice is, more or less, determined by the qualities and condition of each man's material body, inherited from his an-
cestors and variously affected throughout his past life by

the accidents of the material environment. The material environment, on the other hand, can to some extent be modified and reshaped by human will. So it is by this continual interplay between the material processes of the earthly environment and the voluntary choices of men that the texture of history is woven. The result of a critical campaign on which a nation's destiny depends for centuries to come, may itself largely depend upon the weather. Those who planned in 1917 the Passchendaele operations of horrible memory could not foresee the endless rain. The material processes (except in so far as man can affect them) are held to correspond exactly with God's will: the rain of Passchendaele was, as the established phrase has it, an " act of God ": the voluntary choices of men are largely made in opposition to God's will or in disregard of it. Yet both together determine the course of history. This certainly gives rise to a problem.

There are people, impressed by certain still very questionable theories put forward recently by some scientists, that there is an indeterminateness in the ultimate constituents of matter which allows an individual choice comparable to free will in man, or adopting one of the older panpsychic views of nature, who may object that the line drawn between conscious living beings and inanimate matter is unjustified: no matter is really inanimate. This objection will not bear examination. If indeed electrons, or whatever the ultimate constituents of matter may be, can choose individually, as man can, whether they will conform to the divine will or not, it is true that the sum total of their choices — whether in the movement of planets or in the weather — might not correspond with the divine will any more than human society does. But while Christians feel that they express something true when they speak of God being grieved when men choose evil, we have not yet reached the point of thinking it quite natural that God should be annoyed by one of those depressions moving up from the Atlantic, when he particularly wanted the weather in the British Isles to be fine. Or should God will the coming of an epidemic, it is difficult to think of the bacilli, even though they are unquestionably animate beings, hesitating whether or not to obey the divine impulsion.

Whatever the ultimate constitution of matter may be, we do inevitably in practice distinguish between inanimate nature, whose movements are characterized by mechanical uniformities, and the spiritual beings which have a power of choice — the non-human animal kingdom occupying a somewhat problematic position in between. Possibly some dogs may be capable of choosing between pleasure and duty, but we can hardly imagine an oyster ever doing so. Wherever there is no power for such a choice, movements must conform to a pattern which God prescribed for the universe when he created it, the alternative supposition, that the Creator is liable to be surprised at the way the order of things he established works out, being so fantastic that it could be entertained by no one, except perhaps some modern professors of theology.

The philosophy of Nicolai Hartmann is attracting attention at the present moment. Since his construction of the universe is atheistical, it is not likely to command the assent of Christians; but I believe Hartmann to be altogether right, against all who would blur the distinction between purposive human action and the movements of inanimate nature, in maintaining that purposive action, drawn forward to a value in front of it, is essentially different from the causality of movement in the world outside man, where matter is pushed by force from behind. Man alone, Hartmann says, in all the universe, has this power of free decision — " an infinitesimal drop of real purposive activity in a vast ocean of unpurposive causality " (*Ethik*, 2nd edition, 1935, page 188).

Of course, if we believe that non-human nature suffered corruption at the fall, in the way a theology now largely abandoned once supposed, it would be consistent to say that its physical processes to some extent may not now correspond with the divine will. It is, however, difficult to make sense of such a view today when we know that the processes of nature on the planet before the appearance of man showed no superiority to the processes we see today. But even if the belief in such corruption were true, it would make no difference to the argument. The proposition before us is that God's will is perfectly done in the processes of sub-human nature, so far as they are not interfered with by the wrong volitions of finite spiritual creatures. If sub-human nature is now corrupt in consequence of the fall, that is just a case of interference. To put the thing shortly, every movement of matter is caused, on the theistic supposition, by a will, or a conjunction of wills. If one of the wills coming in is that of a finite creature, it may have the power, by God's allowance, of deflecting the subsequent course of things from what is good. If, however, there is no finite will behind the movement — as there is none, so far as we know, behind the movements of a star or of the weather [1] — then the only will behind the movement is that of the original Creator, which has worked, without interference by any other will, through all the processes of nature leading up to it, and God wills only the best possible.

The gravity of the problem comes from the faith essential to Christianity — essential, one would think, to all

---

[1] Though Dante apparently thought that the Devil had some power over the weather (*Purgatorio*, 5:112-114) — a supposition which may sometimes seem in the British Isles to be almost forced upon us.

theism — that God, though the course of history is to a large extent contrary to his will, is nevertheless somehow the Lord of History. He sets limits to what the opposition can accomplish — unbreakable banks, as it were, within which the torrent, chafe and toss it never so wildly, is forced in the end to go where God intends. In the Old Testament we see this lordship of God secured by God's using the material processes of the world, which he manipulates without any possible opposition, in order to set a limit to the godless will of men. Pharaoh's voluntary choice is to pursue and destroy the Israelites; he is allowed to carry it out up to a point; then the Red Sea miraculously opens to allow the Israelites to escape and closes again upon the Egyptians. Sennacherib's voluntary choice is to subjugate the kingdom of Judah; he is allowed to carry it out up to a point, then, before he can take Jerusalem, the angel of the Lord brings physical death upon a great part of his army.

So far as the course of history is determined by material events in man's environment or in his physical body, independently of his will, and these material events are regarded as "acts of God" by which God checks and controls the effects of human choice, a problem is presented for which Christian thought has attempted two different solutions. It is common ground for both that the material event comes in at the precise moment required to meet the acts of human choice, to further or thwart each act, according as God wills. Along the whole course of history the material events willed by God must be a series which is exactly adapted to the other series constituted by acts of human will. If a bullet did not kill Napoleon in one of his early battles it cannot be regarded by a Christian as a mere accident that the position which Napoleon took up on the field was never in the line of a bullet's trajectory: it

must have been God's will that Napoleon should survive
and influence the course of history in the way he did. But
how is this exact correspondence between the two series
brought about? It is to this question that Christian
thought has given two different answers.

On one view, the processes of material nature follow
unvarying laws, except in so far as they are interfered with
by human (or animal) volition; the weather today, for
instance, is a consequence of the movements of particles
in space which have gone on ever since the earth came into
being, according to statical, dynamical and kinetic laws
which admit of no breach, so that any mathematician who
had had complete knowledge of the condition of the solar
system a million million years ago could have calculated
beforehand infallibly what the weather would be in Surrey
on June 16, 1937. For the weather to be different today
something would have had to be different in the nebula
from which the solar system came. If, therefore, the
weather today corresponds by God's will with the spiritual
needs of the human persons affected by it — ruining, it
may be, the hay of a particular farmer, for his soul's proba-
tion or discipline, or turning to sunshine in answer to his
prayer — that can only be because God foresaw from eternity what every human volition would be and arranged the
universe from the beginning so that its material processes
should work out in exact correspondence.

Note that this does not necessarily involve any belief in
the mechanical determinism, postulated by some scientists,
as the ultimate truth of the universe, as more than a con-
venient aspect of it. Even if all the processes of nature are
conceived as immediate workings of the divine will, the
problem is there, so long as God is held to work all through
in accordance with a pattern of uniformities adopted from
the beginning and never modified. The crucial question

is not, What is the ultimate nature of physical causation?
but, Does God know beforehand what all the voluntary
choices of men are going to be? Of course, if one could
hold the extreme view of divine determination, so that
everything that happened, not only the processes of inanimate nature, but the volitions of spiritual beings, evil volitions as well as good volitions, were acts of God, it would
be no problem how the processes of inanimate nature and
the volitions fitted together; it would all be one divine plan
determined from the beginning. But such a view would
make it impossible to contrast a Kingdom of God with a
state of the world in which God's will is only partially
done. God's will would be perfectly accomplished in
everything, good and evil alike. It has, however, been
held by many people — and is, I believe, the approved belief in Roman Catholic theology — that it is not necessary
for the choices of spiritual beings to be determined by God
in order that he should have perfect knowledge beforehand
what they are going to be. Evil volitions indeed could in
no sense be acts of his; yet they are embraced, according to
this view, in his foreknowledge. And if from all eternity
he has known what every volition of every one of his spiritual creatures is going to be, he could so determine the
original qualities and disposition of matter that its processes would work out exactly to correspond. There would
be no need for him ever to modify his plan, ever to depart
from the uniformities of its pattern.

On the other view, the supposition that God foreknows
the free volitions of his rational creatures is rejected. If
it is really still undecided, we are told, what I am going to
choose, God cannot know what it will be. If God knows
what it will be, it is not really undecided, and if it is not
really undecided, my act cannot be free. Some very emi-
nent Christian thinkers in our time have taken this view

— James Ward, for instance, in his Gifford Lectures. It seems to be that of the present Dean of St. Paul's in his recent book *The Purpose of God*. But if you take this view, you cannot possibly both suppose that the series of material events on earth, so far as not interfered with by man, follows, by unvarying laws, from the distribution of matter in the universe a million million years ago and at the same time hold that God is the Lord of History. For the human acts which, on this view, God could not foresee, would continually bring about spiritual conditions with which the material events in the environment did not fit. An earthquake might come according to predetermined laws of matter just at a moment when human volitions had brought about a situation rich with possibilities for the future and throw history out of the line which God desired it now to follow. The view, then, that God does not fore-know the free choices of men and is nevertheless the Lord of History makes it necessary to suppose that events in the material world are not rigidly determined according to a preordained pattern, but may be modified and adapted by God to correspond with the situations brought about by human volitions. When, in this view, rain comes as an answer to a prayer, which God could not have foreseen, it is because an innumerable number of particles in the atmosphere have been made, by God's will, to swerve from the course they would have taken if governed only by the laws of matter in motion.

Theists, who believe in a Creator, seem logically shut up to one or other of these views, unless they think that the Creator launched a world whose course he had either no intention or no power to control. It is easy, of course, to say that you accept neither one nor the other of them, if you like to continue in a nice comfortable notional fog, perfectly satisfied with phrases, without the trouble of thinking out what they imply.

William James, one of those philosophers who have held most strongly that God does not foreknow the choices of men, explained how God might nevertheless be the Lord of History by the analogy of a supreme chess-player playing with an inferior player. The supreme chess-player does not know beforehand what move his opponent will make, but he knows that, whatever moves his opponent makes, he will be able to win the game in the way he designs. The analogy, however, seems somewhat halting. God, on the supposition just taken note of, is not bound to the rules of any game. He is supposed by sovereign will to check human purposes at any point he desires by manipulating material events. It is as if the inferior player were playing against an antagonist who could counter a move by moving a piece in disregard of the rules, just as he pleased. Against such an antagonist there could be no question of victory.

There are probably many people to whom this view of God modifying the process of material events is inacceptable, but who do not find a difficulty in believing that God acts upon the minds and souls of men, sometimes leaving them free to make choices in opposition to his will, sometimes causing them by sovereign power to decide in the way he determined. " The king's heart is in the hand of the Lord as the water-courses: he turneth it whithersoever he will " (Proverbs 21:1). And it might be argued that, even if the sequence of material events, so far as not interfered with by men, follows a course rigidly fixed from the beginning, God can nevertheless be the Lord of History because he can always counter wrong acts of choice on the part of men by making them afterwards will differently, or by causing certain other men to will in such a way as to frustrate the volitions of the wicked. God at particular moments of history, in accordance with his plan, can raise up men into whose hearts he puts such thoughts, volitions, and emotions that the conduct of great masses of men is affected by them — a Constantine, a Francis, a Luther, a John Wesley, or, when it is his will to direct the course of political and national history, a Washington, a Napoleon, a Bismarck. It would not then be necessary to suppose that the course of a bullet in one of Napoleon's early battles had been made supernaturally to swerve, because Napoleon had placed himself in the line of its natural trajectory; God, we should hold, knowing what line a bullet must take, by the unvarying laws of matter in motion, so ruled the volitions of Napoleon that Napoleon never placed himself in any bullet's way. Even if the processes of material nature take a course rigidly determined by natural law from the beginning, God, by intervening, as he wills, in the volitions of men, can adjust history continuously, in spite of volitions which he could not foresee, to correspond with his general design.

That is perhaps the prevalent view, where it is held that God cannot foresee men's free volitions; but I would question whether, in that case, it is really enough, if God is to be the Lord of History, to suppose that God can modify indefinitely, as he chooses, the processes of men's souls, the processes of the material environment being rigidly determined from the beginning. History is made to so large an extent by material events which cannot be affected at all by human volition — the weather and so on — that we must either, I think, supposing these events to be fixed from the beginning, believe that God does foreknow the free choices of men, or we must suppose that he retains his right to modify and deflect the course of material events, according to the choices which men make.

In any case, what we see when we speak of " history," is this continuous process of human lives, directed partly by circumstances outside man's control, but very largely by human acts of choice; and of these acts of choice, a very large proportion, we recognize, are made in opposition to God, or in disregard of him. This gives us the Kingdom of Evil. For the wrong volitions are not simply isolated acts of the persons willing, but they form a concatenation, each wrong volition disposing the person who makes it to further wrong volitions, and having effects in his social environment, disposing other persons to similar wrong volitions. Such wrong volitions in the mass may form customs, institutions, social atmospheres of evil character, which will surround everyone born into the society from his earliest moments, enslave him to standards of conduct and value completely discordant with the divine — a Kingdom of Evil from which it may be difficult for any individual, even with the best will, wholly to emancipate himself. " The whole world lieth in the Evil One " (1 John 5:19). It may be questioned whether the evangelist when he represents Satan as saying to the Lord, after he had set before him the kingdoms of the world, " All this power is delivered unto me: and to whomsoever I will, I give it," supposed the Evil One, in that statement at any rate, to have spoken in his character of liar.

And what of the Kingdom of God? One thing which serious students of early Christianity now, I think, universally recognize is that the connotation of this phrase is essentially eschatological. What the Kingdom is we are told in the Lord's Prayer. It is the coming in of a state of things different from the present state of things on earth. Today God's will is not done on earth as it is in heaven: then it will be done. The Kingdom will come in by some display of God's power and glory, which all men, whatever their wills may be, will not be able to help seeing. Already that same power and glory was giving, here and there, when Jesus was on earth, evidence of itself in the casting out of devils by Jesus. Jesus embodied the power which would transform the earth.

Nineteen hundred years of Christian history have gone by since Jesus spoke, and God's will is as far as ever from being done on earth as it is in heaven. A problem of the Kingdom of God and history can hardly have presented itself 1,900 years ago, when the Kingdom was expected within the lifetime of men who had listened to the Lord. Now we look at a stretch of 1,900 years and forecast an indefinite stretch of years still to come. If the promise " Lo, I come quickly " might mean after 1,900 years — it might mean after 19,000 years or 190,000 years. For us then there is a problem of the relation of the Kingdom of God to this series of events on the planet. With regard to this we have to recognize differences of opinion among Christians. It would seem to me that in any case the eschatological character of the Kingdom stands fast. Human history on the planet is moving to an end in which the divine society which perfectly corresponds with the will of God in love and blessedness will be there, a present reality, and the Kingdom of Evil be something past and done with. Human history has a meaning just because it is moving to such a consummation. Hebraic religion — meaning both Christianity and Judaism — is distinguished, alike from the Indian religions and from the world-view of Greco-Roman thought, by the value it assigns to time. Both for Greek philosophy and for Indian speculation the time-process is an eternal circular recurrence, leading nowhere. If this is so, it is really not worth while being very much concerned with anything that happens in time: it makes no difference in the long run.

" All is change; yet need we not fear any novelty; all is the wonted round; nay, even the apportionments equal. . . . All comes to stench and refuse at last. . . . All things are alike — familiar, fleeting, foul: everything is as it was in the days of the dead and buried . . . Anon earth will cover us all; then earth in its turn will change; then the resultant of the change; then the resultant of the resultant, and so on *ad infinitum*. . . . How silly and strange to think anything in life wonderful! " [2]

The only wise thing is to escape, so far as possible, in spirit from the time-process, to find salvation in the identification of oneself with eternal unchanging ideas, as in Greek philosophy, or with a static reality behind the appearances of the world, as in Indian mysticism.

In the religion of the Old Testament, God is not a static reality, but some One who does " mighty works " in the time-process, beginning with the mighty act of creation. We do not know for certain how soon the definite conception of a world-plan, leading up to a cosmic consummation, arose in Israel. Possibly it arose first in Persian Zoroastrianism and passed from the Persians to the Jews. Among the Jews the idea of a scheme of ages, ending in the establishment of the Kingdom of God, was a characteristic of the apocalyptic literature and was thenceforward a firm constituent of Judaism; but the oldest apocalyptic books, Daniel and Enoch, are not earlier than the first half of the second century B.C., whereas a quotation from the Greek historian Theopompus seems to prove that such an idea was established among the Persians as early at least as the fourth century B.C. But if it was the Zoroastrians who first had a definite scheme of successive world periods, with, at the end of them, a final triumph of good and abolition of evil, an eternal state of bliss for the righteous, the Jews will have adopted the conception because there was a profound affinity between such a conception and their own inherited view of the world. Already in the first chapter

---

[2] *Marcus Aurelius,* trans. Gerald H. Rendell, Macmillan & Co.

of Isaiah, which is, I think, left to the original eighth century prophet even by those critics who make the greater
part of our book of Isaiah consist of later writings, there is
the expectation of a divine judgment which will restore
the nation to a state of ideal righteousness. If we also
allow to the original Isaiah the description of the coming
kingdom of the ideal Davidic king in chapter 11, we have
the anticipation at that date in Israel of a miraculous transformation of animal nature in the days of the coming king,
making dangerous beasts harmless, which is analogous to
transformations of nature envisaged in the Zoroastrian
hope. The now prevalent view of scholars seems to be that
this document is not earlier than the Exile.[3] Even so, it
might be earlier than the fourth century, the date of our
earliest evidence for the Zoroastrian scheme. It is to be
noted also that those who take away chapter 11 from the
original Isaiah admit that they do not do so on any decisive
linguistic evidence.

Hebraic religion and Zoroastrian religion, these two
alone among ancient religions, Archbishop Söderblom
said,[4] stand for a view of the time-process which makes
it end in a Kingdom of God. Events in time had, for this
view, a significance which they could not have for Greek
or Indian thought: " Something *happens* in what happens." Hebrews and Persians agreed in their outlook,
because they both had a conception of God which made
righteous will the essence of his being. To emphasize will
is to emphasize time because acts are done in time. Analo-
gously, on the side of man, what is required is not con-
templative absorption in timeless ideas of static being, but
a correspondence of the human will with the divine will

---

[3] W. O. E. Oesterley and Theodore H. Robinson, *An Introduction to
the Books of the Old Testament*, S.P.C.K. page 247.
[4] Hastings, *Encyclopedia of Religion and Ethics*, i, page 210.

in righteous actions. "Not every one that saith unto me Lord, Lord . . . but he that doeth the will of my Father which is in heaven." With this goes a recognition of the value of the individual, since each occupies a unique place in the time-process, and is never repeated: the individual is no mere example of a universal type. The acts of particular individuals at particular moments of the time-process — Moses, Zoroaster — make a difference to the whole subsequent extent of the process, and thus, although the acts themselves fall into an ever-receding past, they may have eternal value. Jesus, for Christian belief, divides human history into B.C. and A.D.

If this is so, we must strongly repudiate such a view as Inge's, which minimizes the significance of time for the spiritual life and tells us that the blessedness into which man can enter should not be looked upon as anything future. I believe Inge to be in regard to this view Neoplatonic and Vedantic, not Christian. It may be a question how far the future blessedness is itself in time. One thing is certainly true: even if the future blessedness of the glorified community is a succession in time, that blessedness cannot be realized under earthly conditions. It can never be realized on earth as it is in heaven. Its coming implies that the whole earthly order of things, the physical world as we know it, comes to an end, or is left behind. It can be no part of earthly history. Then the question arises, What end are we to expect to human life on this planet? Will it peter out on a dying globe, without ever reaching a higher degree of happiness and goodness than today? Will it be abruptly broken off by God's destroying the present physical order and establishing the divine community in bliss, as all the first Christians believed? Will there be some kind of millennium, a state of society in which there is a provisional and partial realization of the Kingdom, so far as it is possible under earthly conditions of space and time, a kingdom of limited duration, a prelude to the heavenly eternal state, as many early Christians believed?   The petition in the Lord's Prayer, with its apparent insistence upon a difference between heaven and earth and its anticipation of God's will being done in *both,* might seem to support the hope of an earthly millennium.   On the other hand it seems possible to understand the phrase " on earth " as a quasi-poetical way of saying " in human society," and the petition might seem to find its fulfilment in the glorified society of redeemed men in heaven, in which there will be a perfect accomplishment of God's will such as today is seen not on earth but in heaven.

Whenever the main stress is laid upon " building Jerusalem in England's green and pleasant land," the Christian attitude to the world is abandoned.   If that were the main hope of the church, it would exhibit the same deficiency as the non-Christian optimistic humanitarian hope — the belief in a progress of mankind on earth terminating in a condition of comfort and dignity in which the last generations of the human race will pass their lives, till life on the planet becomes impossible from physical changes. It has been often pointed out that the relative happiness of the final generations of mankind upon earth cannot be held an adequate compensation for the sufferings and evils undergone by preceding generations of mankind during, perhaps, a million years — a happiness in which none of those dead generations participate.

According to the true Christian hope, blessedness must be just as obtainable by the men of every preceding generation as it might be by those who live after a new Jerusalem has been built on earth.   This implies the other-worldly hope, the hope whose anchor is in the beyond.   The passage of humanity, so looked at, appears not as a passage along the line of earthly history, to an ultimate goal on earth, but as a passage *across* the line of earthly history, the earth being only a platform which each generation crosses obliquely from birth to its entrance, individual by individual, into the unseen world, the world always there beside the visible one. The formation of the divine community in that unseen world is the supreme hope, in comparison with which everything which happens on this temporal platform, now or in the future, is of minor importance: *there* is the Eternal City toward which our faces are set. That city will embrace equally all men who find salvation at whatever moment of earthly history they may have crossed the platform; the Eternal City was as near to the men of two thousand years ago as it will be to the last generation which will inhabit the globe. It would change the character of Christianity fundamentally if we eliminated from it that attitude to the world which is expressed in the early literature of the church by such phrases as " Here we have no abiding city," or by the description of Christians on this earth as " sojourners and pilgrims."

This means that when we speak of the time-process having a significance, in the Christian view of things, because it leads up to a great and final consummation, there is a possibility of misunderstanding. It does not mean that in the time-process there is a regular evolutionary progress of which the final phase is the natural outcome, all previous phases having value solely as leading up to the last. The time-process has value for the Christian all along because all along it affords the platform, on which men are prepared, or prepare themselves, individually for entrance into the divine community in the unseen world always close at hand. And the final consummation, when it comes, will not be simply the outcome of an earthly process. It will be the manifestation of the sons of God — the sons of God who had been gathered into the community throughout all the ages past and are now revealed in glory. It will be the harvest of the past, not only something new.

Here comes in for Christian thought the problem, What value is then to be assigned to history on this planet? A one-sided insistence upon the other-worldly character of Christianity, upon the conception " sojourners and pilgrims " has sometimes led to the answer, " The value or interest of earthly history is *nil.*" The Kingdom of God, the preparation of men by God's working in their hearts, for the heavenly community, is wholly apart from the course of history made by human volitions, largely bad volitions. To try to improve conditions on earth — on the temporary and perishable platform — is really not worth while. On the other hand the idea, solidly established in the Old Testament, of Jehovah governing the course of history, bringing the children of Israel from Egypt and the Philistines from Caphtor, has also entered into the Christian body of ideas. The course of history, as we have seen, is determined only in part by human volitions; it is also determined by physical events, not controllable by man, and believed to be absolutely controlled by God's will. And even in regard to human volitions, while some are regarded as left free by God to oppose him, some are held to be inspired or directed by him. Christians therefore have been fain to see in history a working of God alongside of human volitions. But is it possible to distinguish, when we look at past and present history, what is due to God's working and what is due to human volitions?

To begin with, we certainly see striking through political, social, economic history, to some extent influencing the course of political, social, economic history, movements of a distinctly religious character, in which the influence of particular persons is predominant. Where such

a religious movement appears to be a new manifestation
and energizing of the Spirit of Christ, a Christian would
certainly say that here the Kingdom of God is active in the
world, and he would regard the influence exerted by saints
and prophets as the power of God working through the
human spirit. But when we try to trace the Kingdom of
God in political, social, or economic changes it is a much
more questionable matter.

One idea which has oddly prevailed among Christians
is that a nation's power and success in the conflict with
other nations is an index of God's approval. " Die Welt-
geschichte ist das Weltgericht." This, of course, is taken
from the Old Testament — " Righteousness exalteth a nation." It belongs to the same system of belief which embraced the conviction that individually righteousness was
always rewarded by prosperity in this life. Already in the
Old Testament the difficulty of maintaining this belief, in
view of the facts of the world, was becoming grievously
felt, as we know by the book of Job. In Christian times
the idea has been given up, as regards individuals: a Christian's faith is not usually tried because he sees a scoundrel
make a fortune or a good man die of a long and painful dis-
ease. But, strangely enough, many Christians have held
fast to a view analogous to that of Job's friends in regard
to *nations*. They have found it impossible to believe that
a God-fearing nation can come to grief or an unjustly ag-
gressive nation get its desire. It was on such a supposition
that some Englishmen said in the late war that they could
no longer go on believing in God if the Germans won, and
some Germans apparently did give up their belief in God
because the Germans did not win. In truth there seems
no reason why a distinction should be made between the
worldly success of an unscrupulous rogue and the worldly
success of an unscrupulous nation. Both are the result of

wrong human volitions which God allows to attain their purpose.

Perhaps two reasons may be discerned why people are led to make a distinction. One is the truth that certain kinds of vice do weaken the fiber of a nation and certain qualities, ordinarily esteemed virtuous, are necessary for its success — discipline, courage, endurance, political sagacity. But this is just as true of the successful individual villain. A financier who dies in possession of a vast fortune will probably have the virtues of industry, self-control, and abstinence from the more tumultuous pleasures, but his hard, selfish heart may make him a less pleasing man in God's sight than the poor unthrifty wastrel who dies in the gutter. Another reason may be that nations, as this-worldly entities, are not held to have, as nations, any future in the other world. While the success of an individual villain may be contemplated with equanimity because it is believed that he will be sorry for it in hell, there is no hell for nations, and it is therefore felt that national misdoing must be punished on earth, or not at all, and, if it is not punished at all, God is not a God of justice.

Whatever God's providential rule implies, it obviously does not involve any correspondence between piety or moral goodness and the acquirement of power and riches, either in the case of individuals or in that of nations. But we may surely trace it whenever we recognize good — not only religious good, but good of all kinds. Any Christian view of the world must hold that men's normal perception of values is largely true. Beauty, as discerned by artist or poet, is a real good; peaceable order in society is a real good; sufficient food and clothing and leisure is a real good. So far as the course of events in the world enables any man to enjoy such goods, he may thank God for them. He will rightly take his opportunity to enjoy them not as something accidental, but as intended for him by God's personal love, and he will believe that the course of events was somehow ruled by God in order that he, and other men, might enjoy them. The course of events will have been in large part determined by human volitions, but he will believe that, so far as those volitions were good, they were due to the work of God in men's hearts, and that God simultaneously stopped such bad volitions from taking effect, as would have prevented the good he enjoys from coming to him.

The sequence of events on earth is woven of good and evil. All good must come from God, whether it comes through human volitions or through fine weather. We say of the evil in the world that God does not *cause* it, but *permits* it, though this " permits " raises the insoluble problem of the relation between finite will and the Infinite will. In this sense, at any rate, we may maintain that pain and the deprivation of desirable good are not according to God's will — that, taken by themselves, they do not show God's purpose. They may form part of a whole which, as a whole, corresponds with God's purpose, because that whole contains a richer good, with the pain in it, than could have been realized without the pain. But when we see a piece of good, we see there a piece of God's final purpose realized. Supposing we are watching an artist paint a picture, we may see him put in some detail — let us say a flower — which, in itself, is beautiful; there we see already manifest a bit of the beauty which the artist designs for his picture as a whole. We may also see him put in some tract of color which by itself is ugly, but which, in the completed design, will contribute to a greater beauty in the whole than could have been brought about, if that tract of color had not been there. We can see the purpose of the artist in the flower; we cannot see it in the ugly tract of color. That shows how we may read a sense into a strange phrase of the Old Testament — that God " does not willingly afflict the children of men "; when we see men receive happiness from God, we see a bit of God's final will realized; when we see men receive affliction from God, we do not see the character, as it will be ultimately revealed, of God's will.

The good which comes to men through the course of events is thus not merely preparatory for the realization of God's purpose at the end of time, but is a bit of God's final purpose already there. My enjoyment of a beautiful sunset is good, taken by itself; it does not draw its value from some ulterior purpose to which it contributes. All through the course of history, in among all the evil things, men are thus always receiving bits of positive good from God — good partial and often transitory under earthly conditions, but nevertheless real good, instalments of God's ultimate purpose, which is directed to men's goodness and joy. It is true that our judgment is very fallible in discerning what is good and what is evil; we often make mistakes. A nation may render thanks to God in a *Te Deum* for an unjust and cruel victory. Yet to suppose that men are quite incapable of seeing the good in what are really good gifts of God would be to make nonsense of all Christian conceptions of the life of men on earth.

While, however, all good comes from God and its coming is due to his providential government of the world process, the New Testament draws a distinction between goods which belong exclusively to the earthly life and the " Kingdom of God." " Seek ye first the Kingdom of God, and these things " (earthly goods) " shall be added unto you." Such things as food and clothing, we are to understand, although they are given by God's loving care, as part of the furnishings of life on earth, are not included in the " Kingdom." The " Kingdom " is the coming in of the

eternal. Human spirits have a life which reaches beyond
bodily death and so far as they here on earth make themselves fit for the divine society of heaven, or experience that
power of God, working in them, which even here produces
in them volitions, feelings, apprehensions which belong to
the eternal life, the Kingdom of God is already, to that extent, here. And if the transient goods, given by God, are
not included in the Kingdom, *gratitude* for the transient
goods, as a response of the human spirit to God's love, no
doubt *is* included. " The Kingdom of God is righteousness and peace and joy in the Holy Ghost " (Romans
14:17) .

Professor Karl Heim, in his recent volume *Jesus der
Weltvollender,* has emphasized the import of the Christian
belief that in the risen and exalted Jesus that transformation of human life into a new mode of being, immune from
death and unrestricted by the laws of earthly matter, which
is implied in the final coming of the Kingdom, has already
taken place, and in so far as Jesus is personally active in
the world today, we have an earnest of God's crowning act
of redemption.

Already, on earth, those who have received by regeneration the life of Christ — the same life as that which will
animate the perfected divine community — form by that
very fact a community. The church is the special sphere,
throughout earthly history, of the Kingdom. The church
on earth *is* the divine community in process of being made.
It is thus essentially different from all earthly communities,
such as nation or state, belonging to the world which passes
away. The community of the really regenerate, by the
activities of those who constitute it in the earthly sphere,
to some extent influences the course of historical events.
It is, though not belonging to this world, a factor in history.
Through it the Kingdom of God intervenes in the series of

human volitions. We must, of course, beware of identify-
ing the community of the really regenerate, whose contours
are not discernible by human eyes, with any ecclesiastical
organization. Some ecclesiastical organization, some rational contrivance, some institution of government with
recognized office-bearers, is quite necessary in order to
maintain, nourish and propagate the life of the regenerate
community; but the ecclesiastical oganization is not identical with that community; sometimes it takes on forms
which thwart and hamper, instead of helping, the life of
the community. The activities of churchmen in history
have too often belonged rather to the Kingdom of Evil than
to the Kingdom of God.

It is by asking how far they minister to good or to
evil that we must judge of institutions, customs, societies,
whether they are of God or not. Signal among human
institutions on earth are the family and the national state.
If affectionate cooperation between men, if civil peace, are
goods, the family and the state, by means of which men
enjoy these goods, must be part of the purpose of God.
If these things are good here and now, apart from any ulterior good for which they may serve, we have in them instalments of God's loving purpose for men already realized.
When the leaders of the early Christian church laid it
down that the imperial government was ordained of God
and bore the sword of God, it was because that government
secured civil peace, and civil peace was a good — an earthly
good, no doubt, a good far inferior to the heavenly Kingdom, but still a real good. But although peace and fellowship were goods here and now, apart from any ulterior
goods to which they ministered, they also had value as
preparations for the greater good of the heavenly community. For if the ultimate good of mankind is social,
salvation consisting in being a member of the divine com-

munity, the exercise of man's social nature on earth may train him for the perfect fellowship on beyond. Earth offers a number of frames within which men's social nature may be exercised — the family and the state perhaps the two most important. The frames are temporary, destined some day to be broken up, as part of the world which is passing away; the characters formed, the "souls made" within them, endure.

The family, the state, are means to this real good, and they are "ordained of God" just in so far as they serve effectively as such means. The family seems something more fundamental than the state. The words of Jesus which rule out for all time any sexual relation among his followers except in monogamous marriage may be held to make marriage an institution which throughout all subsequent human history must be regarded as of God. This may be because the constitution of man is essentially such that the sexual relation can never be clean, when once men have reached a certain degree of moral sensibility, unless it is accompanied by a personal devotion, a consecration to mutual unselfish service, impossible outside monogamy. Yet even if the family is a divine institution, Christians were taught to regard its claims upon them as limited; since it was the means to a good only fully realized in the divine society, the Kingdom of God, the claims of the family might in certain circumstances rightly be set aside in the interests of the Kingdom. "Let me first go bid them farewell, which are at home at my house." "No man, having put his hand to the plough, and looking back, is fit for the Kingdom of God." "If any man come to me, and hate not his father and mother and wife and children and brethren and sisters, he cannot be my disciple." The authorities of the state were ordained by God, as the means to civil peace, but Christians were instructed to disobey and defy the state when its commands clashed with loyalty to the King-dom. How far the existing authority in any state today is to be recognized by Christians as ordained of God should be decided simply by the consideration how far a greater good is to be secured in each case by obedience to that au-thority or by disobeying it. If men ever have to choose be-tween fighting for their national state and helping to bring in some super-national organization of human society, in which there would be a better realization of fellowship among men on the globe, Christians would have no ground for regarding their national authorities as specially or-dained by God. On the other hand, so long as the alter-native to national government in any country is anarchy, Christians may rightly hold that loyalty to the state is loy-alty to God. At the time when St. Paul wrote Romans 13, the only alternative to the imperial Roman government was anarchy.

God, then, must be held the Lord of History, in so far as he limits the effects following from wrong human volitions and in so far as the course of events brings good, spiritual good or earthly good, to men. He is also the Lord of His-tory, because history must end at whatever time, according to the eternal purpose, he wills that it should end. But we should beware of supposing that it is possible for us to trace any progressive approximation in the course of his-tory to the Kingdom of God. The idea of a progressive ap-proximation came in only with the general idea of evolu-tion in the nineteenth century. It may be that if an earthly, partial and provisional, realization of the Kingdom ever comes about under present conditions of space and time and mortality, it will be possible, looking back, to see how the successive epochs of past history led up to it. But we cannot expect to see such progress from our present stand-point. The early Christian church had no thought of such progressive approximation. Things on earth, they believed, would grow worse and worse, till after the great tribulation and the reign of Antichrist the Lord suddenly returned in power. There should be nothing to disturb Christian faith if we see our present European civilization enter into a period of vastly increased evils — war, tyranny, moral disintegration.

> Nathless, discern'd may be,
> By listeners at the doors of destiny,
> The fly-wheel swift and still
> Of God's incessant will,
> Mighty to keep in bound, tho' powerless to quell,
> The amorous and vehement drift of man's herd to hell.
> > (Coventry Patmore, " Crest and Gulf "
> > in the *Unknown Eros*.)

If then the hope of Christians should be anchored in the unseen world, in the heavenly perfection of the divine society, and if there can be no assurance that things upon earth will grow any better before the end of history comes, what should be the attitude of Christians to this-worldly goods — ordered government, social justice, public health, national advance, fellowship overriding class distinctions, art, literature, science? Is it worth while for Christians to devote time and energy to such objects, instead of spending them in preparing themselves for the world beyond and in laboring to bring others into vital connection with Christ?

The answer surely must be that there *is* a danger of the interest of the church being diverted from its true end to the improvement of earthly conditions. Sometimes this has happened. This danger may be recognized and it may still be true that Christians should do what in them lies to further this-worldly goods. Their course is indicated by the two apparently contradictory sayings, attributed to the Lord, " Labor not for the meat which perisheth, but for that meat which endureth unto everlasting life." " I have compassion on the multitude, because they have nothing to eat, and if I send them away fasting to their own houses, they will faint by the way. Give ye them to eat." All the goods mentioned just now may be put in the same class as bread, the meat which perisheth; they are goods which the Lord would not see the multitude go without, because, lacking them, their life in this world is painful or impoverished. Temporal goods may be less important than eternal goods, but unless the church shows the world that God loves it by interesting itself in men's temporal goods, it will hardly persuade the world to believe in the greater goods which God's love offers. Thus, so far from there always being a conflict between interest in men's temporal, and interest in men's eternal, good, it may often be that to show interest in men's temporal good is the best means of leading them to seek their eternal good. What relative proportion of time and energy ought to be devoted by each individual Christian to increasing earthly good and what proportion to spiritual activities, religious in the special sense, would of course differ according to his individual vocation. Specialized functions in particular members of the Body may not represent the proper balance of activities in the church as a whole.

In the endeavor to improve earthly conditions, Christians can have no assurance, as has been said, that earthly conditions will actually become better before the end of history. On the other hand, there is nothing to forbid a hope that they may become increasingly better. There is no reason to suppose that attempts to bring about a juster, a happier, a wiser world are necessarily condemned beforehand to futility. Just as God makes the future of an individual largely depend upon his own free volitions, so it may be that God will make the future of mankind on the planet largely depend on the sum total of human free volitions. Mankind might really bring in a millennial state upon the globe — a state in which men predominantly did God's will and loved their neighbors as themselves — if men, in their multitudes, willed that such a state should exist. No man who seeks to bring larger numbers of men to such a mind knows how far his success may not go. The future is open before us, not shut. Our assured hope at any rate must rest, not on any earthly kingdom, but on the glorified state of the divine community in heaven. The millennial earthly kingdom is a possibility; it is right to strive for it, so far as we have any power to influence men's minds and actions. It is the heavenly hope which is essential to Christianity.

THE KINGDOM OF GOD AND HISTORY

by

Eugene W. Lyman

THE KINGDOM OF GOD AND HISTORY

I

THE problem of the world's history has again become central for human thought, as it was at the end of the ancient world. The judgment is rapidly gaining ground that we are at the end of one of the great periods of civilization and in the midst of a crisis in which civilization itself, and the spiritual values which give meaning to existence, are at stake. At such a juncture a fresh comprehension of the nature and meaning of history becomes imperative if we are not to find ourselves being carried away as with a flood with no hope that the work of our hands may be established.

This problem of the world's history is peculiarly Christianity's problem, for it has been a dominant characteristic of the Hebrew-Christian religion to interpret human existence in terms of history, instead of in terms of nature as did the Greeks. The great Christian doctrines of creation, providence, and redemption have always involved the subordination of nature to history, and the conserving and constructive work of Christianity at the end of the ancient world was conditioned to an important degree by the philosophy of history wrought out by Augustine in his *City of God.*

It would be unwisdom, however, to seek for a close parallelism between the end of the ancient world and the modern crisis. The characteristics of the ancient and the modern periods are widely different. At the end of the ancient period it was a single vast empire which was decaying, and which the cultural cosmopolitanism of the elite was impotent to preserve. In modern European-American civilization the predominant forces have been individualism and nationalism. Into the ancient period Christianity had come as a spiritual leaven whose power to shape history did not clearly emerge till the period's close. In the modern period Christianity — after its long ascendancy during the medieval period, in the course of which its spiritual authority became partly secularized — is finding its spiritual authority challenged by secular forces, which even undertake to supersede Christianity. In fact it is not only the conflict of secular forces with each other which has brought civilization to its present crisis. The crisis is deepened by the antagonism between Christian principles and motives, sometimes in secular guise, and purely secular forces.

But different as are the situations which we find when we compare the end of the ancient world with the modern crisis, the broad likeness remains significant. There is the same need for a religious solution of a world problem insoluble without religion. And there is the same need, if Christianity is to be the source of the religious solution, that it have an adequate philosophy of history. It is the object of this article to contribute toward a clarifying of the Christian philosophy of history, in the face of the present crisis, by a comparison of that philosophy with a view of history which has interacted with it in various ways during the modern period, namely, the evolutionary optimistic view.

This view may be defined as the belief that a general natural law of development has controlled human history, has been the underlying cause of human progress, and is an adequate basis for the continuance of that progress through an indefinite time to come. Thus the essence of the view is a fusion between the idea of progress and the idea of development. These two ideas, while congenial in many respects, notoriously have sprung from two different movements in the modern period. The idea of progress is the product of eighteenth century rationalism, and was bound up in its origin with the mechanical conception of physical nature, and with the idea of universal reason in the field of human nature. This latter idea, in turn, was modified by empiricism and utilitarianism in such a way as to foster belief in the rapid educability and even perfectibility of man. In this setting the idea was one suited to promote movements of radical reform and of revolution. The idea of development, on the other hand, was propagated by the romantic movement which set in towards the end of the eighteenth century in reaction against rationalism, and it became the organizing idea for the modern study of history which expanded so rapidly in the nineteenth century.

The idea of development as a universal law, however, has also had direct rootage in natural science through the Darwinian doctrine of evolution. And since the days of Herbert Spencer this scientific idea of development has been blended with the idea of progress. The result has been the type of evolutionary optimism characteristic of individualistic liberalism. Spencer, indeed, first derived his theory of natural development from reading Lyell's *Geology;* but it was Darwin's work which gave to his theory a firm scientific basis. Thus Spencer was led to the view that human institutions are the product of slow growth, instead of being based, according to the widely prevailing conception, upon a social compact. At the same time he retained the individualistic conception of free competition in economic life, the laissez faire doctrine of the functions of government, and the faith in progress which individualistic liberalism had developed in England.

This combination of the idea of the growth of institutions with the individualistic conception of their essential character has tended to blunt the reformist connotations which the idea of progress previously had contained. In its particular form it has led to the view that progress will come to pass slowly but surely, no matter what ends are pursued by individuals or social groups. Political states may practice power politics and individuals may conduct business for profit only, without reference to the welfare of mankind; yet the general law of development is such that human progress will go forward and the civilization of each century will surpass that which has gone before. Thus when the natural laws which the laissez faire doctrine of political economy holds to be adequate for securing economic justice and general human welfare are made continuous with the laws of biological evolution, there results the view that the evolutionary process as a whole makes progress inevitable throughout an indefinite future time.

The social consequences of this type of evolutionary optimism have been very grave. Beyond question the individualism and nationalism of the modern period have brought with them a great expansion of human power, but the view that the control of this power could be left to the natural processes of evolution has contributed much toward bringing to pass the present historical crisis. Concerning the injurious consequences of this view let me quote the words of Professor John Dewey:

I doubt [he writes] if the whole history of mankind shows any more vicious and demoralizing ethic than the recent widespread belief that each of us, as individuals and as classes, might safely and complacently devote ourselves to increasing our own possessions, material, intellectual, and artistic, because progress was inevitable anyhow.[1]

[1] *The Philosophy of John Dewey,* ed. by J. Ratner.

The consequences of this type of evolutionary optimism for the individual spiritual life have also been seriously limiting and impoverishing. It is true that in the utilitarian ethic which has prevailed in individualistic liberalism the Christian valuation of personality has persisted in the doctrine that " everyone is to count for one " in determining human welfare; but the eudaemonism of the utilitarian ethic has lowered the quality and weakened the energy of its motivation as compared with Christian devotion to eternal values. It is also true that the agnosticism in regard to metaphysical optimism has carried with it a higher appreciation of the religious attitude than was characteristic of eighteenth century rationalism in its more radical form. This was certainly the case with Herbert Spencer. His doctrine of the Unknowable required a reverent attitude toward the ultimate mystery of existence. This reverent attitude may be sustained by symbolical expressions of Ultimate Existence provided the symbols are always recognized to be utterly inadequate. Thus he wrote:

Perhaps the constant formation of such symbols and the constant rejection of them as inadequate, may be hereafter, as it has hitherto been, a means of discipline. Perpetually to construct ideas requiring the utmost stretch of our faculties and perpetually to find that such ideas must be abandoned as futile imaginations, may realize to us more fully than any other course, the greatness of that which we vainly strive to grasp. Such efforts and failures may serve to maintain in our minds a due sense of the incommensurable difference between the conditioned and the unconditioned.[2]

It was doubtless due in large measure to Spencer's widespread influence that " a reverent agnosticism " was a satisfying religious attitude for many minds which, in the

2 *First Principles* (1864) , p. 113.

latter half of the nineteenth century, were relinquishing traditional beliefs under the impact of Darwinism and the philosophy of evolution. When this agnosticism was linked with the belief that evolution inevitably produced progress, there resulted a pale equivalent for a teleological view of nature and history. Indeed, John Fiske, who did so much to popularize evolutionary philosophy in religious circles, always insisted that Spencer's own thought was essentially theistic. Nevertheless there was little in the religious side of this evolutionary optimism to fulfill man's deeper longings for eternal reality and for spiritual transformation, or to motivate him for resisting the mounting evils of economic individualism and unrestrained nationalism.

But there is another type of the evolutionary optimistic view of history which springs more directly from the modern historical movement itself, instead of from the doctrine of evolution as it was shaped from natural science. This type of evolutionary optimism resulted from a fusion of the idea of development and the idea of progress on the basis of monistic idealism. From the days of the Italian philosopher Vico certain thinkers had cherished the ambition to subject human relations to a scientific treatment analogous to that which had won such signal success in the realm of physical nature.[3] This ambition Vico sought to fulfill in his *Scienza Nuova*[4] by the aid of the idea of development. In this work the philosopher represented divine Providence as the governing power in the history of mankind, and demonstrated the formation, development and decay of nations as realizations of ideas pre-

[3] Cf. the full title of Hume's great work, *Treatise of Human Nature, being an attempt to introduce the experimental method of reasoning into moral subjects.*

[4] 1725. Vico's works had little influence until they were translated into French a century later.

existing in the divine mind. It was this idea of development which rendered the romantic reaction against eighteenth century rationalism so successful in the field of
history.

The first expression of this reaction was Lessing's epoch-
making little treatise, *The Education of the Human Race*
(1780). Here the idea of development is applied to
revelation. As education guides the growth of the individual, so revelation by successive stages secures the moral
progress of the race. All great religions play some part in
this development, but no positive religion is final, not even
the Christian. Each religion is worthy to be cherished,
and at the same time its teachings should be translated into
truths of reason. It is not, however, a conception of limitless progress which Lessing here teaches, for progressive
revelation has its definite goal in a " new eternal gospel."
The religious enthusiasts of the thirteenth and fourteenth
centuries, Lessing thinks, had glimpsed a truth in their
doctrine of the three ages of the world, of which the New
Covenant introduced by Christianity was the second.
They erred chiefly in announcing that the third age, that
of the Holy Spirit, was close at hand. But Providence, advancing slowly but surely, will establish the eternal gospel
when love shall be the universal motive and supply its own
reward.

The idea of development was much more fully elabo-
rated by Herder [5] and was directly fused with the idea of
progress; this fusion was given a monistic basis through
Herder's interpretation of Spinoza. As the romantic
movement rejected the realism of Kant's thought, which
was bound up with the doctrine of the thing-in-itself, a
thoroughgoing monistic idealism became the ground for

[5] Herder (1744-1803) has often been called " the father of German
Romanticism."

this form of evolutionary optimism. The guiding idea for Herder's conception of historical development was the idea of humanity. This gave him the conception that progress did not consist in advancing towards a utopia but in the indefinite expansion and realization of the possibilities of human nature. At the same time the idea of the mind of a people was very significant in shaping Herder's conception of historical development, and through this idea the growing nationalism of the modern period gained important philosophical support.

Still stronger support to nationalism was supplied by this philosophy of history as it was given its most influential form by Hegel. For Hegel the state was the highest form of objective mind, which is the Absolute as it embodies itself in the institutions of history. Yet Hegel's theory of development guarantees eternal progress, since each higher unity which results from his dialectic law becomes the starting-point for still further developments. Thus the doctrine of absolute national sovereignty is combined with the doctrine of eternal progress by means of an idealistic evolutionary law.

The significance of this idealistic type of evolutionary optimism appears, first, in its contrast to the first type which is based on a combination of Darwinism and individualistic liberalism. Both types emphasize the view that human institutions are the result of processes of growth, but for the idealistic type social institutions and historical traditions have much greater importance and value. Likewise for this type cultural and spiritual forces play a leading role such as cannot be assigned to them on the basis of biological evolution supplemented by the so-called natural laws of political economy.

In consequence this idealistic conception of historical development has fostered a much stronger social emphasis than has the naturalistic conception of the Spencerian type and has had an important constructive, if also conservative influence upon, political and social life and religious thought. This result can be seen in Great Britain in the influence of Coleridge, who mediated this idealistic conception in its pre-Hegelian form, and also in the subsequent influence of British idealism. Indeed, it was this idealistic conception of development that formed the chief source of the doctrine of the immanence of God, by which the skeptical effects of Darwinism were overcome, and by which many were inspired to active participation in social reform.

On the other hand, this idealistic conception of development has tended to rationalize much in history which the Christian conscience and ethical idealism in general feel bound to condemn. Indeed, under the leadership of Hegel this conception became the vehicle of a new rationalism, according to which historical growth itself means spiritual progress and every historical development is a phase in the realization of Absolute Reason. This historical relativism has brought with it an ethical relativism according to which the existing social structure becomes the chief determiner of ethical obligation instead of being subjected to criticisms from a transcendent ethical and spiritual source. (Cf. F. H. Bradley's expression of the basis of moral judgment as " my station and its duties.") And one of the most dangerous rationalizations effected by this philosophy of history is the sanction, already noted, which it has given to the principle of nationalism.

Alongside of this type of evolutionary optimism based on monistic realism there has arisen another type which has resulted from the voluntaristic movement in philosophic thought, combined with Darwinism. This type has found its characteristic expression in the doctrines of

Nietzsche. The voluntaristic movement has been able to do justice to the irrational elements in experience which monistic idealism has been bound to rationalize. In fact, in the thought of Schopenhauer the irrational elements completely dominate the rational in the form of a metaphysics of blind will and a pessimistic view of human existence. But Nietzsche, though a disciple of Schopenhauer, could not accept this pessimism, and on the basis of the Darwinian doctrine of evolution through the struggle for existence, together with a complete rejection — indeed, inversion — of Christian values, arrived at an optimistic view which made the supreme principle in human history the will to power.

Here the democratic conceptions, which accompany Darwinism in the first type discussed, entirely disappear, and the masses are regarded as the soil on which supermen are to develop a higher mode of existence. On the other hand, an individualistic form of aristocratic theory is arrived at, since the genius, who is Nietzsche's prototype for the Superman, in the hard and ruthless exercise of the will to power to which ideally he is bound, can scarcely make common cause with his fellow geniuses.

Nietzsche's ideal of the superman made him scornful of the philistine bourgeois virtues of contemporary nationalism and militarism; indeed he taught that, far from making patriotism one's supreme loyalty, one should aspire to be a good European and work for the amalgamation of nations. Yet since the will to power as the ultimate metaphysical truth yields no definite standards, it has been almost inevitable that it should be combined with nationalism and treated as a vindication of power politics. Indeed, when voluntarism becomes divorced from Christian ethics and principles of reason alike, it becomes the natural ally of the fascist state. (Cf. the influence of Sorel upon Mussolini.)

Notwithstanding Nietzsche's atheism and his doctrine of Antichrist, there is a religious aspect to Nietzsche's view of history. This can be seen in his exaltation of the Dionysiac over the Apollonian elements of culture and in his prophetic figure of Zarathustra. If there is no God to worship there is the ideal of transcending man to which one can give one's supreme devotion, and there is the hope of a glorious future which one can worship. There is, however, a nemesis which pursues this form of evolutionary optimism; for Nietzsche ends by adopting the doctrine of eternal recurrence, and he escapes the pessimism which that doctrine has always evoked only by his sheer voluntarism. One can say *da capo* to the whole world drama and welcome its inevitable re-enaction.

There is one more type of the evolutionary optimistic view of history which must engage our attention. It is based upon a biological rather than an idealistic conception of the law of development, but it combines with this Darwinian basis the positivistic faith in social science, and conceptions of social solidarity which derive both from positivism and from monistic idealism; and it gives a central place also to the voluntaristic principle, thereby strengthening the reformist motive and the faith in progress. The optimism of this view, accordingly, rests upon a pragmatic evolutionary positivism, and its most characteristic expression is to be found in the philosophy of Professor John Dewey. Kindred teachings are those of the more purely positivistic thinker, E. Durkheim, and of the English realist, S. Alexander; but it is Dewey's philosophy which is especially under consideration here.

Dewey first espoused Hegelian absolute idealism, and

though he has since become a thoroughgoing naturalist and a pluralist, he still shows the Hegelian influence in his optimistic view of man's relation to " the whole ": [6]

Every act may carry within itself a consoling and supporting consciousness of the whole to which it belongs and which in some sense belongs to it. With responsibility for the intelligent determination of particular acts may go a joyful emancipation from the burden of responsibility for the whole which sustains them, giving them their final outcome and quality.

Dewey was also early impressed with Comtean ideas of social solidarity as over against the individualism of British empiricism. And through Comte, as well as directly through Hegel, the idealistic conception of development exerted its influence upon Dewey's thought; for as J. B. Bury tells us, Vico, Herder, and Hegel were being diligently studied in France at the time when Comte was forming his philosophy.[7]

But Dewey came to feel it to be a scandal that one method should be used in the natural sciences and another method in ethics; and since for his thought the natural sciences establish the Darwinian theory of evolution and the biological view of man, the naturalistic conception of

[6] Cf. *Experience and Nature,* chap. X, and *Human Nature and Conduct,* part IV, section IX.

[7] Comte's philosophy of history was pre-Darwinian, but it was strongly influenced by the advance already being made in biological science. This influence reinforced his preference for " organic," in contrast to " critical " periods in history, which was shown in his high esteem for the medieval period and the Roman Catholic Church. His famous " Law of the three stages," through which human culture must pass — the theological, the metaphysical, and the positive stages — meant for him that the metaphysical stage was critical, and that the positive stage must be organic, as the theological stage had been. Moreover, he gave finality to the positive stage. This suggests that the law of the three stages, expressed earlier by the economist Turgot (cf. Theodore Merz, *History of European Thought in the Nineteenth Century,* vol. IV, p. 483 f.n.) is a secularized form of the doctrine of the medieval enthusiasts concerning the three ages, to which Lessing refers (see above).

human development came to displace, in principle, the idealistic conception. On the other hand, the voluntaristic trend in modern philosophy has been potent in Dewey's thought, particularly under the influence of William James, and has resulted in his pragmatic and instrumentalist view of human intelligence and his reformist attitude towards society. Thus Dewey criticizes both traditional empiricism and traditional intellectualism as " otiose," and combines the biological view of man with belief in progress.

Another link between ethics and the natural sciences in Dewey's thought is the influence of technology upon the actual course of modern society and the potentialities of technology as the supreme instrument of progress. Technology has enormously advanced the subduing of nature to human interests, which suggests that by analogous scientific methods human affairs may be brought under intelligent control and human progress be rendered secure and rapid.[8]

If one asks by what standards progress is to be judged and its promotion guided, this form of pragmatic evolutionary philosophy can only point to the social evolutionary process itself and seek to find its standards there. Hence Dewey, in contrast both to Christianity and idealistic philosophy, insists that " social growth " is the only standard by which ethical and practical issues can be decided. Of course Dewey's emphasis upon intelligent control forbids him to regard social change of whatever sort as involving progress; but the progress will result if technology and social science are used in the service of human values, and these values are the natural interests and

---

[8] Cf. Charles A Beard's introduction to the American edition of J. B. Bury's *The Idea of Progress*, issued in conjunction with Chicago's " Century of Progress Exposition."

desires which arise in the process of social evolution.
To be sure, when concrete problems present themselves
Dewey actually employs the standards, ultimately derived
from Christianity, of the worth of personality, of service to
all mankind, and of fellowship and cooperation, and thus
distinguishes his combination of Darwinism and voluntarism from that of Nietzsche which exalts an aristocratic
will to power to the supreme place. But the thoroughgoing historical and ethical relativism of this philosophy
leaves it defenseless when historical crises break down its
optimism, and when whole nations turn to dictatorships
and will-to-power philosophies for their salvation.

This brief survey of the evolutionary optimistic view of
history is enough to show that it differs in important ways
according to whether it rests on a naturalistic or an idealistic basis, according to whether it takes an individualistic
or an organic view of society, and according to the way in
which the rational and scientific tendency is combined
with the irrational and voluntaristic tendency, or the one
tendency is subordinated to the other. But it shows also a
common characteristic running through all the types. For
each type bases belief in progress upon a natural law of
development, and in order to do this each type is obliged
to derive the standards of progress by circular reasoning
from the developmental process itself. This is the case
whether we consider the school of thought represented by
Spencer, or Hegel, or Nietzsche, or Dewey and Durkheim.
Hence this philosophy of history is rudderless in the midst
of the cross-currents of a tempestuous time. It has, indeed,
sought to compensate itself for this weakness, now by retaining Christian standards of the worth of personality and
the unity of mankind, now by the general religious idea
of divine immanence — or in the case of Nietzsche, by
achieving a certain prophetic religious quality and passion

upon an anti-Christian and atheistic basis. But these compensations are so little grounded in the essential theory of this philosophy of history that its adherents are left in a dilemma between a relativism which will justify each of our conflicting historical forces equally well, and a relapse from optimism to complete pessimism.

II

It is with this philosophy of history, which has sought to combine the idea of a general natural law of development with belief in progress, that we are seeking to compare the Christian interpretation of history. This evolutionary optimistic philosophy has presided over a great expansion of historical knowledge, for which expansion it has been to an important degree responsible. It has also left a deep impress upon modern culture in general and, in diverse forms, has been potent in political and economic life. But as we have seen, it ends by leaving human thought in a dilemma between a relativism which is equally available for any form of power politics or economic exploitation, and a complete pessimism, if absolute ethical and spiritual standards are somehow maintained. We must now go on to ask what bearing the Christian philosophy of history has upon the present crisis in civilization. We have noted how Christian ideas in secularized forms have entered into the foregoing philosophy of history; and we are bound to recognize that modern Christian thought has been influenced in varying degrees by this evolutionary optimistic view. Is the Christian interpretation of history able to transcend the dilemma in which the evolutionary optimistic view leaves us, and to furnish us with the grounds and principles for searching judgments of historical events, for guidance in momentous issues, and for an adequate hope?

There are certain inalienable characteristics of the
Christian interpretation of history which bring it into
decided contrast with the evolutionary optimistic view,
and which give it the capacity to transcend the dilemma
between a rudderless relativism and a complete pessimism.
The first of these characteristics springs directly from the
basic nature of Christianity as ethical monotheism.   It
belongs to the nature of ethical monotheism that history
is grounded in the moral will of God and controlled by it,
and that this moral will of God establishes a covenant relation with his worshipers.   This covenant relation is
initiated through an act of God in history.   Indeed the
beginning of Israel as a nation is the divine act of salvation through which the people of Israel were brought out
of Egypt.   The covenant established by this act of deliver-
ance and at Sinai always implied responsibility to the
moral will of God on the part of the people of Israel.
There was nothing of equal partnership in this covenant
idea; nevertheless it was a covenant between God and
Israel, and in this relation Israel must necessarily bear an
active part.

This covenant idea arose prior to the full realization of
ethical monotheism and is more basic even than the idea
of God as Creator of the ends of the earth.   But the idea
of God as Creator inevitably followed, as prophetic teaching and the tragic experiences of the nation widened its
view of history — followed indeed from the very strength
of the covenant relation.   It was the covenant idea of the
relation between God and his worshipers which distinguished the religion of Israel from the surrounding Semitic
religions with their naturalistic view of the relation between deity and worshipers — a view from which only
prophetism was able to emancipate the religion of Israel
itself.   The covenant relation involved the obligation of

obedience and loyalty to the moral will of God, which demanded righteousness in the life of the nation, and it involved the ingratitude and guilt of any disobedience — "which my covenant they brake, although I was a husband unto them, saith Jehovah." It carried with it the inescapable punishment for unrepentant disobedience and the conception that other nations, themselves not worshipers of the true God, would be instruments for this punishment. It bore fruit in Hosea's message of divine redemptive love because of the unalterable faithfulness of God; in the inwardness and individualism of Jeremiah's religion and his message of a new covenant; and in Second Isaiah's profound conception of Israel as God's chosen servant and an instrument through its sufferings for the redemption of the nations. Thus throughout the prophetic teaching of the Old Testament, history receives its meaning from a series of divine acts in accordance with a covenant relation between God and his worshipers which rests back on God's moral will and in which men bear a responsible and active part.

The ministry of Jesus Christ and the preaching of St. Paul presuppose this interpretation of history and deepen and extend its meaning. Jesus' message of the Kingdom of God issues in his interpretation of his death as the actual instituting of the New Covenant by God. St. Paul justifies his preaching of the gospel to the Gentiles on the ground of the New Covenant which God established through the death of Christ; and his defense of his apostleship is in terms of his being minister of "a new covenant; not of the letter but of the spirit." The whole drama of divine redemption through Christ, as given in the speeches in Acts and in the theology of Hebrews as well as in the Gospels and in the Epistles of St. Paul, is in the framework of a philosophy of history according to which the moral will

of God is in control of all events, but is peculiarly manifested in special divine acts establishing covenant relations
with men. St. Paul indeed extends these relations in principle to all mankind, for through the revelation of God
in creation and through " the law written in their hearts "
all men are responsible to God's righteous will. Yet the
old covenant embodied in the Mosaic law was a peculiar
manifestation both of God's righteousness and his gra-
ciousness, and carried with it a peculiar responsibility on
the part of his chosen people Israel. The consummation
of these covenant relations is the New Covenant whose
content is the gospel of the Kingdom, in which the ultimate
disclosure of God's righteousness and grace is made, and
through which all men may be redeemed into sonship to
God and empowered for the service, and even for the suffering, which the fulfilment of God's moral purpose in
history entails.

A second inalienable characteristic of the Christian interpretation of history is that eternal values have been
made known to men by God, and that these eternal values
are always relevant to history, being the basis of its meaning and establishing the content both of sin and of salvation. It is the eternal justice of God which, in the
preaching of Amos and his followers, is the basis of the
condemnation of all human license and oppression and
of the doom that must fall upon unrepentant Israel. It
is the eternal faithfulness and mercy of God which are
the basis of Hosea's hope for the redemption of the people
of Judah. It is the mysterious union of eternal justice and
eternal mercy in the holiness of God which in Isaiah's
vision gives him his threefold realization of the unclean-
ness of himself and his people, of God's forgiveness of his
iniquity, and of his prophetic mission.

Each of the special divine acts in history involves a further revealing of eternal values with no diminution in the significance of those already revealed. To the prophet of the exile comes the vision of vicarious love. In the person of Jesus Christ, prepared for by all the prophetic revealings that have gone before, there is revealed the religious value which unites all other values — the love for God and man which is God's own active love redeeming man, bringing him into sonship to God and into the Kingdom of God which is righteousness and peace and joy in the Holy Spirit. And when one sees in the establishment of the Christian church, and in other historic events, further divine acts and new revealings of eternal values, these can only be acknowledged when they are in harmony with the supreme religious value which is revealed in Jesus Christ.

From the two foregoing characteristics of the Christian interpretation of history there emerges a third which is no less permanently essential. The Christian view of history is a dynamic one, according to which historic events have positive meaning from the standpoint of eternal values and the transcendent ground of history in God, and according to which historical events receive their ultimate explanation in terms of dynamic agencies.

Historic events, in the Christian view, are not illusory appearances or shadowy and confused expressions of eternal essences which are more real than the events themselves, as Indian and Greek thought has tended to conceive them. Rather, the historic events are the concrete realities with reference to which eternal values are decisive norms, or structural principles, and apart from which those values have only abstract logical significance. Similarly, the conception of the moral will of God as the ultimate ground of history means that it belongs to the very nature of God to create and sustain beings capable of

historic action through purposeful deeds and social relationships.

The most significant aspect of this Christian dynamic
view of history is the dynamic character of the vehicles of
divine revelation. The prophet makes known the will of
God and does so by intervening in historical events. From
the days of Elijah onward the prophets were " troublers of
Israel," and Jesus recognized in the warnings and denun-
ciations of John the Baptist the very spirit and power
of Elijah. We always honor discoverers and teachers of
truth, but the one who single-mindedly and courageously
does the truth always arouses in us something of religious
awe. The prophet is not only an oracle of God; the true
priest was always that. The prophet is also a revealer of
the will of God by historic action. He often struggles
painfully against this necessity for historic action as Jeremiah did, but " the burning fire shut up in his bones "
prevails and breaks forth in prophetic deed.

Here is perhaps the underlying reason for Jesus' adop-
tion of the rôle of Messiah. Though he must transform
the meaning of messiahship, yet he must also embody the
will of God in deed; and without this deed, which included
both the triumphal entry to Jerusalem and the agony of
Gethsemane and of the cross, " the revelation of the mystery " of the gospel would not have been complete.

But the dynamic character of prophetic action is to be
seen also in the fact that the prophet is the founder and
permanent inspirer of a spiritually dynamic community.
From the prophet comes the school of his disciples, who
preserve and edit his writings and themselves have the
prophetic fire.[9] From such a dynamic community exten-

---

[9] Cf. Isa. 8:16–17: " Bind thou up the testimony, seal the law among my
disciples. And I will wait for Jehovah, that hideth his face from the house
of Jacob, and I will look for him."

sive moral and religious reforms have come to pass, such as that embodied in the Deuteronomic law.   But the dynamic character of the prophetic community appears especially in the arising of new prophets, who challenge the institutional and legal results even of the prophetic reforms in the strength of a deeper apprehension of the will of God.   Even John the Baptist, who seems to us so solitary a figure, left behind him a school of disciples, whose later absorption into the Christian community is hinted in the New Testament record.   Jesus' announcement that the Kingdom of God was at hand is chronologically and inseparably linked with the gathering of a group of disciples, to whom he entrusts the continuance of his mission and who become the nucleus of the Christian church.   The missionary preaching of St. Paul, likewise, is inseparable from his founding of churches, without which his gospel of liberty and of the indwelling Spirit of Christ, which transcends all distinctions of race or social status, would have been of no effect.   In the thought of St. Paul Christians cannot be true to the spirit of Christ unless they are members one of another and so are forming a vital organic unity whose bond is love.

A fourth essential characteristic of the Christian interpretation of history and one that gathers up into itself the other three which we have just considered, is its conception of the goal of history in the Kingdom of God.   The idea of the Kingdom of God is absolutely central for the thought of Jesus, and at the same time it was for him so rich and many-sided in its meanings that it has presented several perplexing problems to New Testament scholars. We can speak of it here only in relation to the Christian view of history, and in summary and dogmatic fashion.

The Kingdom of God, in the Christian view of history, is a transcendent-immanent conception and stands for a transcendent-immanent goal. It means always the king-ship and rule *of God,* who both grounds history and tran-scends everything that ever can be expressed in history; and it always means the kingship and rule of God *in his-tory,* thereby determining history's meaning, true direc-tion and goal. Since history is the realm of man's purpose-ful activity and moral responsibility in dependence on the moral will of God, its ultimate explanation can never be in terms of naturalistic determinism but must always be in terms of the activity of the living God — saving men, holding men responsible, judging them and summoning them to repentance, bringing doom upon unrepentant sinfulness, showing mercy and forgiveness in response to repentance and faith, and binding men together in an organic unity in which unrighteousness is divisive, destruc-tive, and brings suffering to others, and in which righteous-ness and love are unifying, upbuilding, and effective for transmuting suffering into redemption. History thus has a direction determined by the eternal values of God's nature and by his active willing toward their realization, and it has a goal in the community of love which is the body of Christ. This goal of the community of love is itself transcendent-immanent. It cannot be completely realized in history, since God and the meaning of his love transcend history, and hence it implies an eternal life which is beyond the bounds of this earthly existence. But no other limits can be placed to its realization in history. There are no concrete evils or forms of sin from which the love of God cannot redeem men through the realizing in history of a community of love.

The Kingdom of God also stands for a reality that is both present and future. This goes with the dynamic conception of history which we have noted in the Chris-tian view. The prophet who makes known the will of

God is also the instrument of God's will in historic action. There is a moral union of his will with God's which means the kingship of God in his heart and life. At the same time he is a forerunner of the Kingdom or the preacher who is summoning men to repentance in preparation for the Kingdom's climactic manifestation. The limiting conceptions for this view that the Kingdom of God is at once future and present are the conception of it as wholly an apocalyptic hope and the conception of it as wholly a present experience of the life eternal — in other words, the conceptions of the Kingdom as wholly supernatural and as purely mystical. But neither of these limiting conceptions is true to the faith in a revelation of God in history. The Kingdom of God must be understood as both present and future if we would grasp the Christian philosophy of history.

Furthermore, the Kingdom of God according to the Christian view of history must be understood as both personal and social in its meaning. It means the personal doing of the will of God from the heart and the blessedness which comes to faith, humility and the childlike spirit, as Jesus taught. It is, as St. Paul taught, "righteousness and peace and joy in the Holy Spirit." At the same time it means the gathering of men into a community whose bond is love. This is an elect community, whose election, however, is not to privilege, but to service. This service must be guided and inspired by Jesus' compassion for the weak, his welcome to the disinherited, his indignation against injustice combined with his summons to humility and to being servants of all, and supremely by his sense of the sovereignty of God's moral will, by his message of the forgiveness which renders the repentant heart forgiving, and by his conviction of the boundless possibilities which open before faith in God.

This community will itself be a dynamic realization of the Kingdom of God in the degree to which it shares St. Paul's vision of a new humanity through a living faith in Christ, since " God was in Christ reconciling the world unto himself." It will be inspired by the apostle's consciousness of being debtor to all men, " both to Greeks and Barbarians, both to the wise and to the foolish." In it there will be diversities of gifts, but all will contribute to an organic unity which is the body of Christ. This community itself, being elected to service, is committed to fulfilling a prophetic function on the world. In the light of the whole Hebrew-Christian philosophy of history this function must include becoming instrumental for the transforming of all social institutions until they become subject to the spirit of Christ.

The four characteristics of the Christian view of history which we have noted bring it into sharp contrast with the evolutionary optimistic view. They present history as grounded in the moral will of God instead of in a natural law of development, whether biological or idealistic. They present the meaning of history in terms of eternal values manifested by special divine acts rather than in terms of essences irrelevant to history, or of natural values which shift with the historic process itself. They do not make human historic action negligible but exalt it, not however in terms of arbitrary will to power, nor of the sufficiency of human purposeful intelligence, but in terms of a responsible dynamic relation to a living divine will. They do not allow an individualistic and an organic view of society to be pitted against each other, but unite them through the conception that men are called to live as children of God and as members one of another. They present the only kind of goal of history which is consistent with acknowledging a cosmical setting and metaphysical basis for history, namely, the transcendent-immanent goal of the Kingdom of God.

Thus the dilemma between complete relativism and complete pessimism, into which the evolutionary optimistic view issues, is overcome. One does not have to acquiesce in a universal relativism which gives a like validation to any and every historical movement, whether nationalism or imperialism, whether democracy, communism, or facism, because one has knowledge of eternal values, relevant to history yet transcending history, by which every historic movement must be judged. One is delivered from an ultimate pessimism, because history springs from God's eternal will to realize these values, because they have been dynamically realized through specific acts of God, and because one may participate in their further realization.

The full expression of the way in which the Christian view of history transcends the evolutionary optimistic view involves the appreciation, and at the same time the transmutation, of certain significant ideas in the latter view. The idea of development, so important for the latter view and for historical method in general, is important also for the Christian view, notwithstanding the fact that it became influential long after the Christian view took shape. For example, if the code of Hammurabi exercised a positive influence upon Hebrew ethics, then it has positive significance for our understanding of God's action in the Hebrew prophetic movement. There are not two histories in the objective sense of the term — one natural and the other supernatural. There is the complex of human events, interacting with the complex of physical events, both being conditioned upon a metaphysical ground. Any valid developmental view of a section of human events has significance for our understanding of God's action within and upon those events. One must not put a premium exclusively on discontinuities for the sake of a religious interpretation of history, any more than one can accept continuity as a dogma. Both continuity and discontinuity are in themselves neutral from the religious point of view. One must take any verified developmental account of events realistically if moral and religious judgments concerning those same events are also to be taken realistically.

Similarly, the view of man presented by biological evolution is relevant to the Christian view of man. True, the genetic account of man does not determine his value or his metaphysical relationships. But scientific anthropology and Christian anthropology deal with the same race of human beings, and scientific anthropology presents conditions with which any significant Christian anthropology will concern itself, just as what we know of man's economic life presents conditions with which Christian ethics must be concerned.

The idea of progress, likewise, should receive positive appreciation in the Christian view of history, though it must have a different interpretation from that given by the evolutionary optimistic philosophy. According to evolutionary optimism the operation of natural law makes progress inevitable in the long run. To be sure, the intelligent effort of man is also requisite. The positivist Guyau declared that the substitution of human providence for the omnipresent influence of divine providence might be given as the formula of progress. But the making of intelligent effort is itself subsumed under evolutionary law. According to the accompanying psychology of this philosophy moral effort is sure to follow where there is sufficient knowledge, and the growth of human knowledge is, at least empirically, well assured. But the link between value and evolutionary process is neither a logical nor a merely natural one. The position to which Huxley, the great expounder of evolution, came in regard to ethics is testimony to this fact. Hence, as we have seen, either evolutionary optimism swings to pessimism or it is obliged to approve whatever human valuations gain a footing in history.

Nevertheless there is a real kinship between the idea of progress and the idea of a purpose of God in history. The latter idea includes the use of human instruments in the positive realization of value. These human instruments — the prophet and the prophetic community — are at once purposeful and dependent upon the moral will of God, and the results of this submission of the human will to the divine will in historic action are cumulative. This is the unmistakable meaning of the prophetic communities and of sacred Scripture. The transcendent relation of the instrument to God must not be separated from the immanent relation of God to his instruments which is cumulative and corporate in its workings. And whenever there is a realization of genuine value as the result of a cumulative process, there is progress so far forth.

The idea of a fulfilment of God's will in history which depended upon a preparation has always been a part of Christian thought. When the idea of development established itself as essential to historical method it became necessary for Christian thought to consider the relation between verified developmental processes and the fulfilment of God's will in history. Any positive connection between a given development and God's will must indeed be a judgment of faith, for it involves an apprehension of eternal values as dynamically made known by God's living will; but it involves the acceptance of the verified development as realistic truth. The Christian thinker and the scientific historian deal with one and the same history in the objective sense of that term.   If the Christian thinker could not discern any cumulative realization of spiritual value in history the result would be a kind of inverted Pelagianism.   One of the evils of Pelagianism was its denial that deeds of will passed over into character.   It is a similar error to suppose that becoming an instrument of God's purpose for the realization of value has no cumulative effects in history.   As a matter of fact the idea of a progressive revelation of God in history has been a great gain for Christian faith, and it in no wise contradicts, but on the contrary implies, the acknowledgment of special divine acts in history.

Thus the Christian view of history is to be clearly differentiated from the " *belief in progress*," — that is, in a natural law which renders progress secure and certain. But it does recognize a progress in the past to which Christian faith itself is indebted, and it includes the hope of progress in the future, because it rests on the faith that men may become instruments of God in the positive and cumulative realization of spiritual value in history.

Certain other aspects of the evolutionary optimistic view of history may be given positive significance when once the essential independence and primacy of the Christian view has been established.   The work of Ernst Troeltsch is very valuable for the right orientation in this respect.   Troeltsch affiliated his thought to Bergson's doctrine of creative evolution, which on the one hand served to strengthen evolutionary optimism, but on the other hand was based on metaphysical intuition.[10] Troeltsch combined elements of Hegelian thought with

10 Bergson has not given us a philosophy of history, though he has approximated to one in *The Two Sources of Morality and Religion*. The too sharp antithesis which he there makes between moral and religious institutions and creative morality and religion Troeltsch could not have accepted.

voluntarism and thus delivered the organic view of society from being a static doctrine. He had a high valuation for the social sciences but gave them a spiritualistic basis over against positivistic naturalism. He established the creative rôle of Christian faith and thought in the shaping of Western institutions of culture, and he maintained the dynamic meaning of Christianity in relation to the future after the war by upholding as a practical goal the ideal of a new cultural synthesis in the West, at the heart of which should be Christian faith. Troeltsch's work is a monumental product of liberal Christian thought and has contributed permanently to the Christian understanding of history. Nevertheless, Troeltsch never quite succeeded in transcending the relativism which haunts a thoroughgoing developmental philosophy, though he wrestled with it over and over again; and he conceived the idea of a new cultural synthesis too facilely, as did all liberal thinkers who espoused the idea in the first three decades of this century. The Christian view of history requires a more thorough independent grounding than Troeltsch gave it, at the same time that it requires the dynamic relevance to history which he so effectively established.

One aspect of the Christian view of history should be especially stressed in face of the present world crisis. It is the aspect in which an elect community is seen to be an essential instrument of the will of the living God. Such a community is elected not to privilege but to service in historic action; in other words it is a prophetic church. It is not a sectarian community, saying " I am of Paul," or " I am of Apollos," or " I am of Cephas," or " I am of Christ." It is the invisible church becoming incarnate in the visible church, through the indwelling spirit of Christ building itself up in love. It does not regard the visible church as a competitor of secular institutions, or as one cultural institution among many, but it insists that the visible church and all cultural institutions must be subject to the transcendent-immanent Kingdom of God. It cannot allow economic institutions or the political states to be laws unto themselves, but must seek an organic society through establishing the ascendancy of spiritual authority based upon the revelation of the will of God in Jesus Christ.

That the church can fulfil a prophetic function is being given awe-inspiring demonstration before our eyes today. The Confessional Church in Germany is being a troubler of the totalitarian state no less truly than Elijah was a troubler of Israel, in the name of the sovereignty of God and the spiritual authority of Christ. Will the prophetic function of the church become the inspiration of all its priestly functions? Will the visible church deliberately nourish prophets who shall be instruments of the moral will of God in historic action? Will the visible church so coherently and effectively express a spiritual authority through its own obedience to the moral will of God that it will bring modern civilization to repentance and mediate to it the regeneration and renewal which it receives itself from the indwelling spirit of Christ? The answers to such questions tremble in the balance in these days. Yet the answers will be fully perceived only by later generations. At all events when we seek to apprehend the Christian interpretation of history in relation to the present world crisis, we are bound to think in terms of longer time-spans than the optimism of both secular and Christian liberalism envisaged in the opening decades of the century; and at the same time we are bound to hold in more vital union the submission to the transcendent will of God and obedience to that will in prophetic historic action on the part of both the individual Christian and the Christian church.

THE KINGDOM OF GOD AND HISTORY

by

PAUL TILLICH

THE KINGDOM OF GOD AND HISTORY

INTRODUCTION

1. THE TASK

THE task with which I have been entrusted is that of giving a religious interpretation of history from the standpoint of the Christian belief in the Kingdom of God. Christian theology, under the influence of Greek thought, has taken almost incredible pains over the problems of the natural, and the moral sphere seen in the light of the Christian faith in God. In the sphere of the Christian interpretation of history, however, in spite of some outstanding individual conceptions, the problem of the *Kingdom of God and History* has received far less attention. This is partly due to the pressure of an ecclesiastical conservatism, which has regarded history as practically consummated in the existence of the church. The opposition of the revolutionary sects, in all the various periods of church history, was not sufficiently strong to break down this barrier. It is only during quite recent years that the question of our historical existence has become central for all vital theological and philosophical thought and discussion. The churches can evade this question only at the cost of a complete withdrawal from the life of the present day. They are summoned to reflect upon the great solutions of their past and to seek for a new solution, expressed in some powerful symbol, which will meet the need of the humanity of the present day in its questionings and its despair.

2. THE WAY

The way to this goal leads through a threefold process of reflection. First of all we need a philosophical and theological clarification of the concepts used. It is obvious that this preparatory stage is of more than merely formal significance. Even the most abstract conception of history, and the most formal presentation of the categories which constitute it, include ultimate philosophical decisions. These, for their part, are dependent on ultimate religious decisions, consequently on religious faith. Thus the preparatory work on the concepts concerned contains, in abstract form, the whole solution.

The second step is the general presentation of the relation between the Kingdom of God and history according to theological principles. Here the task of theology proper outweighs that of philosophy, which is relevant for the first step. Here too, however, it is true that the whole is included in the part. For since theology has to do both with the Logos and with practical life, at least so far as its form and its material are concerned, it is also determined by philosophical and practical decisions.

The third step is the concrete attitude to the historical forces of the present day. Since the only entrance to the interpretation of history is historical action, there is no serious grappling with the problem of history which has not been born out of the necessity for coming to a present historical decision. Philosophical idealism and theological transcendentalism try to conceal this state of affairs. But it comes out clearly in every single interpretation of the historical process, and indeed in every category of interpretation, however abstract it may be. It is therefore more honest and more fruitful to include in the interpretation of history itself the fact that such interpretation is rooted in historical action and, on the other hand, to justify this by means of the actual interpretation.

3. THE STANDPOINT

The practical standpoint presupposed in the following outline and at the same time to be confirmed by it is that of so-called " Religious Socialism." It starts with the insight that the bourgeois-capitalistic epoch of occidental development has reached the stage of a most radical transformation which may mean the end of this epoch altogether. Religious Socialism links this insight, which is being more and more widely acknowledged by people of historical consciousness, with the special conviction that the coming form of human society must be a socialist one if it is to be adequate to the actual necessities as well as to the moral demands of the situation. The religious interpretation of history explained in this article consequently has two roots — a religious-transcendent root, the Christian message of the Kingdom of God, and a political-immanent root, the socialist interpretation of the present. The former supplies the principles and criteria, the latter the material and the concrete application. This bi-polar method is essential for any religious interpretation of history. It does not, however, mean that the theological decisions are subjected to the political ones, neither does it mean that political decision acquires theological dignity. It rather means that the divine claim over the world is not kept within an abstract transcendence but is used for evaluating and molding actual reality. Religious interpretation of history is " *applied theology*," and therefore necessarily bi-polar. Any attempt at eliminating the concrete, political pole entails either the destruction of a true interpretation of history, or a concealment of the latent political attitude which in this case becomes effective unconsciously and without criticism. Interpretation of history is subjected to the same methodological demand as the production of a Christian " world view " or of Christian ethics; there must be the quest for a bi-polar beginning.

PART I: CONCEPTUAL PREPARATION

1. THE CONCEPT OF HISTORY

(1) History is the totality of remembered events, which are determined by free human activity and are important for the life of human groups.

History is *remembered* history. Both in German and in English the word " history " has a twofold meaning: subjective and objective. This suggests the fact that history, in the strict sense of the word, begins as soon as historical consciousness arises, which creates historical tradition. But the converse also is true. Historical consciousness and historical tradition arise as soon as history in the strict sense of the word begins. The subjective and the objective element, memory and event, are inseparable.

History is dependent upon free human activity, but it is not dependent on this *alone*. Nature too has a share in the making of human history, in so far as it creates the geographical, biological and psychological bases for it, and also exercises a constant influence upon human action. But nature itself has no history because it has no freedom. In all nature the existence of things is a necessary result of their essence. In man existence is opposed to his essence. Upon the basis of existence new things happen, which do not follow from essence, but are due to human freedom. Here is the difference between mere becoming and history. (Biological spontaneity may provide a transition from the one to the other, but ultimately it belongs to nature, not to history.)

Among the countless events in which human freedom participates those alone constitute history which stand in relation to the life of human groups. The action of the individual only gains historical significance through his relation to the life of a social group. This is true even when his action takes the form of *separation* from the social group. Even the hermit in his denial of society is related to society. And only through this relation does the life of the hermit as a whole gain historical significance.

(2) Historical groups are all those human groups which on the one hand have the power to exist and to maintain their existence, and on the other hand are the bearers of a definite system of values for the establishment of which the historical group feels responsible. This sense of responsibility is expressed in the form of consciousness of a special vocation.

Every human group may become a " bearer " of history: from the family, by way of the tribe and the nation, perhaps up to a united mankind. Yet mankind as a whole has not hitherto become a " bearer " of history, since it has not achieved a uniform group existence supported by power, nor has it gained a common sense of values.

Historical existence presupposes power, at least the power to exist. Since, however, life only exists while it is growing, the *power of growth* also belongs to historical existence. A group only has the power to exist and to grow in this way if, as a group, it is *united,* that is, when it has the possibility of forming a united political determination. Every living form of power realizes itself in constantly changing discussion with other powers, natural or historical, and out of this the impulse to historical movement is born.

Human freedom implies the consciousness of meaning and value. Accordingly, every historical group feels its existence to be in a special way meaningful and filled with value. No imperialism could develop apart from such a sense of value or of vocation. The nationalism of the Western nations is absolutely bound up with a definite consciousness of vocation.

(3) Historical time is directed time — time with an end, a beginning, and a center, and is consequently *qualitative* time, developing in different periods.

Historical time must be distinguished from physical and biological time. In nature the cyclic movement of time predominates; the end returns to the beginning; nothing essentially *new* takes place. In history directed time breaks through the cyclic movement. Something new takes place and replaces the process of mere repetition. Emergent evolution in the biological realm may be considered as a limited anticipation of the historical newness, limited first by the lack of freedom of decision, second by the fact that with the creation of " man historical " biological evolution seems to have reached its summit and end.

From this it follows that history is not merely a continually flowing stream which can be measured by quantitative standards, but that every historical period has a special quality whose character is dependent upon its significance for the total historical process. Thus for the Christian consciousness the time before and after Christ does not only differ quantitatively but qualitatively. The understanding of the total direction of history is decided by the event in which a human group perceives the meaning of its history. We call it the *center* of history. The character of this center then determines the conception of the *aim* of history, and the center is at the same time decisive for the fixing of the beginning of history, that is, that point in time in which a human group for the first time becomes conscious of its historical character. Thus, for instance, from the Christian point of view, *Christ* is the *center* of history, the realization of his Kingdom is the *end,* and the first expectation of the Kingdom is the *beginning* of history.

Historical time cannot be measured in terms of physical time. Billions of years before and after man appeared on the earth neither continue nor frustrate the meaningful direction of history. Neither the end nor the beginning of history can be designated on the plane of physical time.

(4) *The meaning of history can be found neither in a final stage of historical development — the ultimate fulfilment of all historical potentialities — nor in an infinite approximation to a fulfilment which can never be reached, nor in a continuous change of historical growth and decay as found in nature, nor in a transcendent supra-nature unconnected with history.*

The idea of a final stage in which history has, so to speak, fulfilled its aim contradicts human nature, since in historical man existence is necessarily contrasted with essence. (This is not a natural necessity, but is made necessary by freedom and fate.) Further, the idea of a final stage would exclude all other stages and all generations of men living in them from the meaning of their historical existence.

The idea of progressive approximation to a final fulfilment can only be applied in three directions. First, in the sense of technical progress, which is the original and adequate meaning of this concept; second, in the sense of a progress in political unification, which is to be considered as a consequence of the technical control of mankind over the whole earth; third, in the sense of the gradual humanization of human relationships. But there is no progress with respect to the creative works of culture or with respect to the morality of mankind. The first is impossible because creativity is a matter of grace, not of growth; the second is impossible because morality is a matter of free decision, and consequently not a matter of delivery and tradition. Education can only communicate the standard and level on which moral decisions can be made, not the decisions themselves. Further, it must be said that an infinite approximation to the final fulfilment would replace the fulfilment by the way towards it; and this is ultimately self-contradictory.

The naturalistic interpretation of history, as for example Spengler's theory of cultural circles which grow up and decay, or the nationalistic interpretation of history from the point of view of national growth and decay, reduces history to the level of nature. In both these cases the distinction between what is and what ought to be, between true and false, between good and bad disappears in favor of self-realization, self-expression and power.

History loses its meaning when it is presupposed that its meaning and value are fulfilled in an eternal world of essentialities, which is either entirely severed from historical development or is only accidentally connected with it. Both in the thought of Plato and in that of Neo-Platonism history is thus emptied of content. Both interpret the relation between time and eternity in such a way that what happens in time has no meaning for the eternal at all. Both make nature the pattern of history either in an idealistic or in a mystical form, and both miss the significance of history.

(5) *The ultimate meaning of history is the suprahistorical unification and purification of all elements of preliminary meaning which have become embodied in historical activities and institutions.*

The category of the supra-natural is used to express a closer relationship of the transcendent, ultimate meaning to the immanent, preliminary meaning than the categories eternal and temporal are able to do. The supra-historical is beyond history but it is essentially related to history, while eternity is the mere opposite of time. It is meaningless to speak of the supra-historical in terms of a stage of being, or a form of existence, or something future which is not yet but will be sometime. The transcendent cannot be expressed in terms of being but only in terms of meaning. We understand what is meant by " unconditioned meaning " — for instance, unconditioned good or truth — but we do not understand what is meant by " unconditioned being " because all our thinking is limited to the realm of conditioned beings and its categories.

From this point of view we can affirm only two characteristics of the ultimate meaning of history: it is unification and purification. Unification means that the dispersed embodiments of meaning in historical activities and institutions have an invisible, supra-historical unity, that they belong to an ultimate meaning of which they are radiations. And purification means that the ambiguous embodiment of meaning in historical realities, social and personal, is related to an ultimate meaning in which the ambiguity, the mixture of meaning and distortion of meaning, is overcome by an unambiguous, pure embodiment of meaning.

In so far as this unity and purity lie beyond history we have to state that the meaning of history transcends history. In so far as nothing is contained in this unity and purity, which does not belong to real history and its dispersion and ambiguity, the meaning of history is to be found in history. Both statements are true, but they are true only in connection with each other. In this way historical activity acquires ultimate importance without becoming utopian, and the supra-historical acquires content without becoming mythological.

2. THE CONCEPT OF THE KINGDOM OF GOD

(1) *The Kingdom of God is a symbolic expression of the ultimate meaning of existence. The social and political character of this symbol indicates a special relation between the ultimate meaning of existence and the ultimate meaning of human history.*

It is a symbolic expression for the relationship of the unconditioned meaning of existence to actual existence. It must be symbolic since it is impossible to grasp this relationship directly and unsymbolically. It is, however, a true symbol, i.e., a symbol which irreplaceably stands for what is symbolized. It expresses the majesty, controlling power and distance of the unconditioned meaning of existence with respect to the realm of conditioned meanings. There are other possible symbols for the same relationship taken from different realms of experience. So, for instance, Paul speaks in a more ontological way of the final stage of existence in which " God will be all in all." In John there are more mystical symbols, such as eternal life in Christ, friendship with God. All these symbols have in common the presupposition that being as being is meaningful, while the doctrine of Nirvana sees the ultimate meaning of existence in the dissolution of being.

" Kingdom " is a symbol taken from the social and political sphere. It points more than the other symbols mentioned to the overwhelming importance of human historical life for the ultimate meaning of existence. It suggests that human personality, freedom and community constitute the center of existence, its development and its fulfilment. Consequently this symbol has to be the main tool for a Christian interpretation of history.

The historical relation of the symbol " Kingdom of God " is obvious in the latent contrast implied between the

Kingdom of God and the kingdoms of this world. The Kingdom of God is expected to triumph over the kingdoms of this world; it is a dynamic power acting in history, materializing itself in history although never becoming identical with history.

(2) *The contrast between the Kingdom of God and the kingdoms of this world is expressed most clearly in the assertion that there is a demonic opposition to the Kingdom of God within the realm of human history. History in this way becomes a battlefield of the divine and the demonic.*

The " demonic " is a category which was used for the religious interpretation of history in Persia, in Jewish Apocalypses, in the New Testament, and in the ancient Christian church up to the time of Augustine. Later this category emerged again and again in periods of great historical tension. The loss of it in modern times is connected with the rise of the idea of progress and the destruction of the original Christian interpretation of history. It is understandable that the breakdown of the idea of progress amid the historical catastrophes of the present and recent past has given a new significance to this category. Religious socialism was the first to rediscover and use it. This was possible only because the mythological or ontological sense of the demonic, in which demons are a kind of beings, was sufficiently destroyed, and so the term could be applied to that destructive, blind, chaotic element which is implied in all powerful creating movements and drives them toward final dissolution. While the word " demonic " has this positive and creative connotation, the word " satanic " points to a purely negative principle. The satanic can only be understood as absolute contradiction, while the demonic participates in the divine creative power. Therefore the satanic cannot exist in itself; it needs the positive of which it is contradiction; it has reality only in the reality of the demonic powers which control existence generally, and human existence especially.

When Augustine equates the Kingdom of God with the church and the Kingdom of Satan with the great world empires, he is partly right and partly wrong. He is right in asserting that in principle the church is the representative of the Kingdom of God; he is wrong in overlooking the fact — which as a Catholic he could scarcely help overlooking — that the demonic powers can penetrate into the church itself, both in its doctrines and institutions. He is right to the extent in which he emphasizes the " demonic " element in every political structure of power. He is wrong to the extent in which he neglects the creative significance of the political power for historical existence.

(3) *In the symbol of the Kingdom of God the final victory over the demonic powers in existence generally and in history especially is implied.*

The Kingdom of God is a dynamic conception. It designates the necessity that the ultimate meaning of existence is never given; it acquires reality only in overcoming meaninglessness and the distortion of meaning. " Righteousness, peace and joy," the characteristics of the Kingdom, enclose a possible opposition which is overcome in them. It is not completed but always becoming; not present, neither immanently nor transcendently, but always " at hand." It expresses that " God is a living God," entering history, struggling in history, fulfilling history and is not the unity of eternal essences.

Therefore it is wrong to conceive the Kingdom of God merely as the restoration of the original order which has been destroyed by sin. We know nothing of such an order. It is an abstraction whose roots lie in a static conception of transcendence. The Kingdom of God is, however, not a system of eternal essentialities, whose realization was given in the creation, was lost at the fall, and was regained in redemption. The Kingdom of God is the dynamic fulfilment of the ultimate meaning of existence against the contradictions of existence.

PART II: THE GENERAL CHRISTIAN PRINCIPLES

1. THE KINGDOM OF GOD AS THE MEANING OF HISTORY

(1) *For the Christian consciousness Christ is the center of history. His appearance is interpreted as the " fulness of time," that is, as the fulfilment of all historical preparation.*

In calling Christ the center of history we do not apply a general category to a special case, but we apply a category which is found through the analysis of the significance of Christ (in Christian faith) to Christ; we return to Christ what we have taken from Him. For in Christ, namely in the reality which is contained in different original interpretations in the New Testament, Christianity sees the appearance of the ultimate meaning of life in history. The fact that the Christian nations speak of a period before and a period after Christ shows how deeply Christian consciousness is penetrated by belief in Christ as the center of history.

The center of history is decisive for the beginning and the end of history. From the Christian point of view history has a supra-historical beginning — the fall; and an intra-historical beginning — the rise of the expectation of a redeeming event. History has also a supra-historical end — the final consummation or the parousia of Christ; and it has an intra-historical end — the victory over the anti-divine powers which arise in history, or the reign of Christ. Neither this beginning nor this end can be determined in terms of physical time. We can express them only in symbolic records of the past (Gen. 1–12) and in symbolic interpretations of the future (millenniums).

A specially important category of the New Testament interpretation of history is *Kairos*. It designates the fulfilment of the period of expectation or preparation, and the beginning of the period of reception or fragmentary actualization. The Greek word *Kairos,* which originally only meant without discrimination the " right time," is used in a prophetic interpretation of history for *the* right time in which all time gains its meaning and qualification. The predominance of the logos-doctrine within the Greek church prevented the development of a *kairos*-doctrine, i.e., a Christian interpretation of history.

(2) *The Christian interpretation of history considers the history of mankind ultimately as history of salvation.*

The belief that Christ is the center of history, and that in him the reality of salvation has appeared in history, implies the belief that human history is ultimately to be interpreted in terms of salvation. Salvation means the fulfilment of what existence ought to be by overcoming the destructive, meaning-defying, powers of existence. As in Christian doctrine, Christ is saving man in temporal life as well as beyond temporal life, so the history of salvation is going on in history as well as beyond history. Salvation is actualized in history whenever a demonic power in social or individual existence is overcome by the divine power which has become visible in Christ. And salvation is actualized beyond history in the ultimate unification and purification of meaning.

The human mind is not able to conceive salvation beyond life and history in terms taken from world experience which are technically called " ontic." It can be conceived only in terms of meaning. If ontic terms such as resurrection, immortality, new earth and new heaven are used, they have a symbolic character, since they point to some elements of the ultimate meaning of existence. So, for instance, the symbol of resurrection points to the truth that the totality of personal life, including the human body, belongs to the ultimate meaning of existence. The symbol of a new earth points to the truth that the natural basis of history is not excluded from the ultimate meaning of existence. Hence it follows that the choice of symbols is decisive for truth or error.

Salvation is related to individuals as well as to groups, to mankind as well as to nature, to personalities as well as to institutions. For the problem of history the salvation of groups and institutions is of special importance. It means that the demonic perversion and destruction of groups and institutions is overcome, partially in history, completely beyond history. While the Christian churches in the Catholic period dealt with the salvation of individuals and with the salvation of groups and institutions only with respect to the church itself, and in Protestantism the salvation of groups and institutions is neglected altogether, the post-Protestant period of Christianity probably will deal predominantly with the ultimate meaning and the salvation of groups and institutions. The fact that a religious interpretation of history has become a very urgent problem of applied theology testifies to this.

2. THE KINGDOM OF GOD IN HISTORY

(1) *The realization of the Kingdom of God within history is determined by the history of the church, in part directly through the historical growth of the church itself, and partly indirectly through the conscious or unconscious relation of all history to the history of the church.*

If the meaning of history is salvation, then all history must be related to that course of history in which redemption is prepared and received. The church is the " bearer " of this course of history, both in the stage of preparation and in the stage of deception.

Hence we are justified in calling the church the " bearer " of history. Of course this does not mean that the events of world history have been determined, in an historico-empirical sense, by the synagogue and the Christian churches; only a very small part of mankind, from the point of view of space and time, has any contact with the churches at all, and even where there is contact, or even very close touch, it is truer to say that the secular powers have far more influence on the outward destiny of the churches than the other way round. But the church is more than the Christian churches and their precursors. The church is the community of those partly visible and partly invisible, who live in the light of the ultimate meaning of existence, whether in expectation or in reception. The church, understood in this way, is the power which gives meaning to historical life as a whole.

The meaning of Christian missions is based upon this truth. It is the task of the Christian mission to gather the potential, divided church out of all religions and cultures and to lead it into the actual church, and in so doing to transform potential world history into actual world history to give humanity a unified historical consciousness. This also means that all over the world expectation is to be transformed into reception.

(2) Through Christ as the center of history, history is divided into two main periods: the period of preparation and the period of expectation. In each of these two main periods, however, this division is repeated, in so far as history always has the basic character either of expectation or of reception and fragmentary actualization of a new principle of meaning. The transition from the one to the other may be called a special *Kairos*.

From the standpoint of its ultimate meaning all history is either the preparation for or the reception of the center of history. But the preparation is never merely preparation; it is always also anticipating actualization. If it were not so, all pre-Christian history would be devoid of meaning. But this would be true neither of the prophetic Hebrew stage of preparation nor of the general " sacramental " preparation within paganism.

The vital force of both is drawn from their anticipating reception of the center of history; the Jewish development in direct preparation for its appearance, and the pagan development in indirect preparation create the parallelism of understanding. On the other hand, the post-Christian development is never only reception, since it always contains pagan and Jewish elements of expectation and preparation.

The fundamental division applies also to the two main periods themselves. Each period is subdivided into shorter periods, each with its own center which gives it meaning, its own beginning and end. Periods which seem to be controlled by expectation are succeeded by periods which prove to be a fragmentary actualization. From the sociological point of view this has been described as the rhythm of " critical " and " organic " periods. Even the history of the church often follows this course. But no age is completely lacking in " reception " and none is without an element of " expectation."

For the Christian interpretation of history the centers of particular periods are dependent upon the center of history. This gives the criterion for the interpretation of each center and for historical universal action from every particular center. If the New Testament idea of the *Kairos* is applied within a definite period, it expresses the conviction that that which has appeared once for all in " the fulness of time " has reappeared in a special way as the center of a particular historical period. The unique, non-recurring *Kairos* remains the standard for all the particular forms in which it reappears. For instance, the period preceding the Reformation may be called a period of expectation and anticipating actualization. The appearance of the new interpretation of the center of history by Luther may be called a special *Kairos* (as Luther himself felt), and the Protestant materialization after him may be called a period of reception and fragmentary actualization. In the same way the present period of the decay of liberalism and secularism may be called a period of expectation which perhaps may be followed by a period of reception after the turning-point, the *Kairos,* has occurred. It is exactly this feeling which gave rise to the renewal of the doctrine of *Kairos* by " Religious Socialism." It is impossible to give criteria abstracted from the actual situation by which the existence or non-existence of a special *Kairos* can be judged. It is a matter of the faith of those who act in a special situation; it is a venture which may fail because faith and spiritual power may not be strong enough. The " will of God " in any given historical situation cannot be recognized by general criteria but only by daring faith.

3. SALVATION AND WORLD HISTORY

(1) *For the Christian interpretation of history salvation is the meaning of world history. But salvation is not the same thing as world history. Primarily and above all salvation is judgment passed upon world history.*

The negative presupposition of world history is human freedom with which the symbol of temptation deals, and the emergence of the contradiction between essence and existence which is expressed in the symbol of the Fall. From this presupposition of history there follows the contradiction in which it stands to salvation: salvation is the actual overcoming of the contradiction between essence and existence upon which world history is based.

A direct expression of the contradiction in history is the abuse of power. Power in itself is a structural principle of historical existence. But it is not only in accordance with but also in opposition to the meaning which is to be realized through historical power. It not only fulfils historical vocation but it also betrays it. In so far as all history is a history of struggles for power, salvation is judgment passed on world history. The external expression of this judgment is the destruction of power by power. Hence in the Kingdom of God, the goal of world history, power is only found in absolute unity with love.

(2) *If world history were only opposition to salvation, it would directly destroy itself. It can only exist at all because it is not only judged by salvation but is also supported by it.*

Power cannot exist without a meaning, in the name of which it is power. The values with which power must unite itself are realizations of the meaning of history, moments in the fragmentary actualization of salvation upon which the possibility of power, and therefore of history, are based. The sociological expression for the fact that power needs a meaning, in order to be able to exist, is " ideology." The word " ideology " has acquired a negative sense, challenging the deliberate or unconscious misuse of ideas for the preservation of a power whose existence is threatened. But the thing itself, the combination of power and value, should not be estimated in a merely negative manner; it is the positive foundation of history as a whole.

History is carried by those groups and individuals who represent in their existence a meaning which belongs to the ultimate meaning and is unified and purified in it. As far as salvation is the latent meaning of history those are its real bearers who incorporate and represent in themselves this meaning, either in expectation or in reception. The spirit of salvation radiating from those personalities and groups is the power which again and again overcomes the demonic self-destruction of historical existence. If we call the latent community of those people the invisible church, we must agree with the New Testament in asserting that the church is the real bearer of history. This is not a claim for the empirical churches, but a demand upon them.

It is a general experience that in the moment in which the divine breaks into the temporal and a new *Kairos* is approaching the demonic acquires increased power. It is, however, impossible to derive from this experience a general law of progressive regressive development of universal history. Both judgments, the optimistic as well as the pessimistic, should be avoided.

(3) *As salvation is carrying world history so, on the other hand, world history is the fragmentary actualization of salvation.*

The seriousness and the gravity of human history depends upon the fact that world history is the fragmentary actualization of salvation. Each particular act which is related to the ultimate meaning which has appeared in Christ has infinite significance, because it is the " coming of the Kingdom of God." It is a logical result of their point of view that those who interpret the Kingdom of God in a purely transcendental manner finally come to regard history as a meaningless occupation of man with himself, while the concept of salvation falls away altogether.

The fragmentary actualization of salvation in world history does not mean that salvation can be fulfilled within history. For salvation within history is opposed by destruction; the divine is opposed by the demonic. Salvation is actual within world history to the extent in which the destructive forces are overcome, the power of the demonic is broken, and the final fulfilment of meaning appears. Thus salvation within world history does not remove the conflict between the divine and the demonic.

Accordingly the doctrine of the millennium should not be interpreted as a static final condition, and certainly not in Augustine's sense of the sovereignty of the hierarchy. The millennium should be interpreted as the symbol of the victory over concrete demonic forces within history. The demonic is subdued in actual victories from time to time — but it is not extirpated. When the power of a particular form of the demonic is broken the *kairos* of a particular period is fulfilled. To expect not only that the power of concrete demonic forces will be broken at definite periods in history, but that in some future age the demonic as a whole will be utterly destroyed, is a religious " utopianism " which should be regarded as quite untenable.

The relationship of the fragmentary actualization of salvation in history and its fulfilment in the transcendent unity and purity of meaning cannot be expressed in terms of time and history. Every attempt to do so makes the ultimate meaning a section in the totality of meanings, a history after history, a time after time. History itself can define the supra-historical only in negative terms. Every positive expression is a symbol and has to be understood as such in order to avoid that " transcendent utopianism " which belongs to the distortions of religion and Christianity.

PART III: THE PRESENT TASKS OF THE CHRISTIAN INTERPRETATION OF HISTORY

1. THE SIGNIFICANCE OF THE "PRESENT" FOR THE CHRISTIAN INTERPRETATION OF HISTORY

(1) Historical interpretation is self-reflection on the part of one who is acting historically about the meaning, the purpose and the presuppositions of his historical action. The Christian interpretation of history is the reflection of the Christian who acts as a member of the church about the meaning, the purpose and the presuppositions of his action as a member of the church.

Historical interpretation is *self*-interpretation, that is to say, the historical interpreter must himself be living and acting historically. History cannot be understood from the outside, from the non-historical point of view of the spectator. All historical interpretation contains a concrete historical decision; that is, the spectator's point of view has been abandoned. Historical action is not confined to political action in the narrower sense of the word. All action which aims at the formation of community, however theoretical it may be, is historical action; in the broadest sense of the word it is " political."

The purpose of this process of reflection on the part of one who is acting historically is to help him to perceive the spiritual presuppositions on which his action is based and further, by the " give and take " of discussion with those who hold views, either to justify, or, if necessary, to alter his own basic principles, and thus to give spiritual weight and the power to create community to historical action.

All this also applies to the Christian interpretation of history, which is self-reflection on the spiritual presuppositions of the action of the church; for Christian-historical action is church action. Reflection on the part of one who is acting as a member of the church is reflection upon his spiritual presuppositions, that is, the spiritual principles, the essential philosophical and theological ideas, and the present reality from which his action springs.

Church action flows in two directions: along one channel it seeks to influence the churches which now exist, as historical facts; along the other channel church action is directed towards the historical existence of an epoch as a whole.

(2) All Christian historical action is determined on the one hand by the universal center of history, and on the other by the center of the particular period in which the action takes place. Accordingly, in all Christian historical action the sense of the unique *kairos* is combined with the sense of a special realization of this *kairos;* this also implies that the struggle against the " demonic " forces in general becomes concrete in the struggle against the particular " demonic " phenomena of the present day.

Christian historical action or church action, in the universal sense of the word, is bi-polar: the one pole is the unique (*einmalige*) center of history, the *kairos* in which in principle the ultimate meaning of history has appeared, in which the demonic destruction of history has in principle been broken. The other pole is the actual situation from which the action of the church springs, whether such action is related to the churches themselves or to historical existence as a whole. " Church action," in this sense, may take the form of ecclesiastical politics or the politics of the state, it may be theological or philosophical, artistic or liturgical work, or it may take the form of constructive work in religious or secular communities, education in church or school. Every actual situation from which

Christian historical action proceeds contains a negative and a positive element: the negative element is the special "demonic" phenomenon which is characteristic of a period, and especially of a period of transition, and against which the prophetic struggle of the church must be directed; the positive element is the special promise and the special demand which this situation carries with it, an element which was described by the term *kairos*.

The bi-polarity of Christian historical action, as well as the difference between its two tendencies, is the cause of a whole series of tensions and problems which arise out of a one-sided emphasis on one of these poles or on one of these tendencies. If the unique *kairos* excludes every other, that is, if it denies bi-polarity, then all Christian historical action becomes meaningless: the reality of the Kingdom of God is independent of such action, for it belongs to a sphere beyond and above history (*dialectical theology*). If the individual concrete forms of the *kairos* destroy the unique *kairos*, then the criterion for Christian historical action disappears, and in place of the struggle against the "demonic" we see Christian theology falling a prey to changing forms of the "demonic" (*nationalistic theology*). If one-sided emphasis is laid upon the tendency to concentrate action *within* the church, then world history itself is abandoned, uncriticized, to the dominion of that force which destroys all meaning (*orthodox Lutheran theology*). If one-sided emphasis is laid on Christian historical action outside the church, then church history loses its independence, and in so doing its critical power to give meaning to history as compared with world history (*liberal-reformed and denominational theology*).

Christian historical or ecclesiastical action is carried out either by the church as such, that is, by its official representatives (synods, bishops, clergy, lay people who exercise official ecclesiastical functions), or by members of the church (under some circumstances also outside the organized churches), who act as members of the church but not as representatives of the church. Representative ecclesiastical action may be directed both negatively and positively towards the church itself (creation of confessions or creeds and of constitutions, fight against heresies and wrong conditions), but it can only influence historical existence outside the church negatively, not positively (by revealing the " demonic " forces and their destructive consequences, by forming a critical estimate of ideas and plans in the light of the ultimate standard, but not by fighting for definite philosophical, artistic or political solutions). The positive aspect of historical action outside the church can only be achieved by Christians who are either entirely or in certain definite functions not representative of the church, and who are willing to incur the risk of falling into philosophical and political errors, and of being disowned by the church (Christian philosophers, educationists, politicians, artists, etc.). The Christian interpretation of history which issues from the sphere of concrete historical decisions of this kind has no ecclesiastical or dogmatic significance, but it may have prophetic or theological significance.

2. THE ACTUAL " DEMONIC " FORCES OF THE PRESENT DAY

(1) The fundamental " demonic " phenomenon of the present day is the autonomy of the capitalistic economic system, with all its contradictions, and the mass disintegration and destruction of meaning in all spheres of historical existence which it produces. This " demonic " force has been unmasked in the main by the prophetic spirit outside the church, but this discovery may, and indeed must, be

absorbed into Christian historical categories and developed still further; we should also note that the Christian interpretation of history given in this article owes some of its own vital impulses to this discovery of capitalism as a " demonic " force.

The autonomy of the economic sphere, which is the result of the doctrine of economic liberalism, has had two fundamental results: first of all, it has caused the class struggle which arises inevitably out of the mechanism of an industrial system, which like all other " demonic " forces is quite independent of the moral will of the individual and causes destructive divisions within society, and even within the church.   Second, the economic sphere, which has become autonomous, has brought all the other spheres of human historical life into subjection to itself and has deprived them of independent meaning; thus it has set in motion a great process of mass disintegration, the movement of which is subject to destructive laws.

The socialist movement, and primarily theoretical Marxism, has opened the eyes of Western society to the working of these laws.   The vitally prophetic element in Marxism, under the pressure of the spiritual situation of the nineteenth century, has clothed itself in anti-religious materialistic forms, which are inadequate for what is meant by the idea of socialism.   Under the name of " Religious Socialism " the Christian interpretation of history has set itself the task of expressing the anti-" demonic " criticism of Marxism in the categories of the Christian interpretation of history; the impulse to the discovery of such categories came essentially out of the presence of a socialistic movement with a Marxist interpretation of history: the categories which are expounded in this article have been brought into the sphere of the theological thought of the present day by the urge to unite Christianity and socialism in positive criticism.

The content of the categories of the Christian interpretation of history springs from the prophetic and sectarian
tradition and its reflection on the philosophy of history
throughout the centuries.   Christian theology, which
makes these categories its own, does not support a special
political party, but by making use of the intellectual tool
which a sociological theory has placed at its disposal it has
re-formulated Christian thought on history.   The implicit
political decision which has been made in Religious Socialism cannot become an ecclesiastical decision in the formal
sense of the word.   It must remain a venturesome decision
of some individual members of the church, a decision
which may possibly contain error.   The church, however,
is under obligation to bear formal witness against the destructive consequences of the " demonic " forces of the
present day and their heretical foundations.

(2) The " demonic " force of *nationalism* is dependent
on the " demonic " element in the economic system, yet
at the same time, as a means of mass reintegration, it is to
some extent opposed to it.   At the present time nationalism
is the most evident and the most dangerous incarnation of
the " demonic " principle in general, especially where, as
in various places, it has assumed an explicitly religious
form.   It represents the modern variety of polytheistic
bondage to space and division, and it drives that section of
mankind which has fallen under its sway to historical self-
destruction.

Nationalism means that the natural and historical reality
known as the " nation " is posited as an absolute, that is,
it constitutes the supreme good to all who belong to it.
This also means that all who do not belong to this nation
are excluded from a share in this supreme good.   To the
prophetic view of history the supreme good and the criterion of all historical existence is the Kingdom of God, in
which all national divisions have been removed, but to

nationalism the self-assertion of the nation over against
every other is the supreme good and the criterion by which
human historical existence is measured.   Thus in nationalism the emphasis upon space, characteristic of polytheism,
has been restored, in contrast to the emphasis on time in
prophetic and Christian monotheism.

Nationalism must therefore be described as neo-paganism even when it assumes no explicitly religious form.   In
the countries in which it has assumed a religious form the
Christian and the nationalistic views of history have come
into open conflict, and the church has formally condemned
nationalistic neo-paganism as heretical and " demonic."
The Christian interpretation of history, however, must go
further and reveal the heretically " demonic " character of
the nationalistic system of values as such; above all it must
show that with the elevation of a definite space, of a definite
race, and of a definite nation to the rank of the supreme
good, history as such has been abandoned, spatial coordina-
tion and division have triumphed over temporal direction
towards a goal.

The development of nationalism in the Christian West
is made possible by the division and disintegration introduced by capitalism.   Once the nation had been substi-
tuted for the church as a unifying center, it appeared to
afford the first and the most natural principle of reintegration; this process was hastened by the fact that the church
was utterly incapable of providing such a principle, since
she was weakened by her own divisions and by the fact that
she too was entangled in the net of widespread disintegration.   But this nationalistic form of reintegration, when
regarded from the Christian and the humanistic point of
view (which indeed overlap) , actually represents the most
advanced stage of disintegration.   Nationalism must be unmasked and attacked by those who hold the Christian and

prophetic view of history as a kind of false " prophecy " in the sense of the Old Testament.

(3) The necessity for the reintegration of the masses has led to dictatorial forms of government, in which the " demonic " force of an unrestricted exercise of power drives men into presumption towards God and to destruction of the human values which belong to the Kingdom of God: formal justice, truthfulness and freedom. This is also true of that form of government which, in the name of material justice, has rejected the " demonic " forces of capitalism and nationalism.

Unrestricted exercise of power is a " demonic " temptation which none who possess it can resist. The early church expressed this in its condemnation of the Roman Empire. Henceforward tyranny has always evoked the opposition of Christian historical thought. Tyranny is presumption towards God and oppression of man. Hence it falls under the condemnation of that combination of love and power represented by the idea of the Kingdom of God.

This is the case, in the first place, when dictatorship is surrounded by a halo of an almost religious kind, or when it proceeds to attack the church. The deification of the dictator, whether as the representative of the ruling power or as an individual, the interference of the state, with its totalitarian claims, with the sphere of religion, the quasi-religious character of its decrees imposed like taboos, the enforced conformity of the church to the state, or its destruction, and the creation of martyrs in the narrower sense of the word — these are the anti-Christian implications of the exercise of absolute power. They force the churches into a campaign of direct resistance, and they provoke those who hold the Christian and prophetic view of history to make a vigorous protest against this " demonic " exercise of power.

But there is another series of results of the unrestricted exercise of power which also comes under the condemnation of the idea of the Kingdom of God, i.e., the destruction of human values by tyranny. The Christian doctrine of man, as having been created in the image of God, as well as the doctrine of Christ as the Logos, means that Christianity is responsible for the human values: i.e., formal judicial justice, which is the prophetic standard for the estimate of a political power; truthfulness, to deny which the New Testament regards as an evident sign of the satanic principle; and freedom, that is, the recognition of human dignity or, in Christian terms, the fact that every human being is potentially a child of God. To the satanic principle also the New Testament ascribes all actions which injure this human dignity, whether they touch man's mental life (by putting a " stumbling-block " in his way) or his physical life (by murder) .

The deliberate renewal of these " demonic " forces whose power has already been broken by Christianity in principle, and is being hotly contested by Christian humanism in practice, constitutes the third outstanding " sign of the times." Even the Bolshevist dictatorship, in spite of the fact that it is fighting against capitalistic and nationalistic disintegration in the name of material justice, is of this " demonic " character. Thus the protagonists of the Christian view of history are called to bear their testimony in the name of the idea of the Kingdom of God, in the midst of their present historical existence, against capitalism, from the point of view of its content; against nationalism, on account of its content and its way of exercising authority, and against Bolshevism on account of its way of exercising authority.

3. THE "KAIROS" OF THE PRESENT MOMENT

(1) The " demonic," in a threefold form, threatens to destroy our present historical existence. From the human point of view the tragic element in this situation drives those who study history from the Christian point of view to inquire into the positive meaning of these events, that is, the *kairos* immanent within the present moment in history. In accordance with the double direction of ecclesiastical action a double answer is required: one which is given within the church and one outside the borders of the church.

A situation is tragic in which the very elements which are most valuable by their very value drive it to self-destruction. This is the case with the humanistic element contained in capitalism, as well as with the purpose of reintegration which is contained in nationalism, and with the expectation of justice which is contained in Bolshevism. All three in a tragic fate contradict their own original intention and are driving society as a whole, in the Christian West, towards self-destruction. The protagonists of the Christian view of history cannot prevent this tragic fate, but they can and should show clearly the *kairos* which is being fulfilled within this process of self-destruction, that is, the positive principle which is giving meaning to this development. In so doing they will provide the present action of the church with a concrete criterion and a concrete aim for the future.

(2) The fact that our present historical existence is menaced means that the church is called to reformulate the universal reintegrating principle which Christianity contains, the center of history as a whole and as a present center. This means *negatively* the freeing of the church from her entanglement with the disintegrating powers of

the present and the past; *positively* it means the preparation of a new historical existence through the action of the church.

It is impossible in this connection to point to all the consequences which spring from the Christian action of the church within her own borders. Some points only can be mentioned here.

First of all we must understand the radical nature of the present process of historical self-destruction, in which the churches also are involved. This applies to Protestantism in particular, with its lack of power to provide a reintegrating principle for the masses. We must reckon with the possibility that, in the narrower sense of the word, the Protestant period of the church may already be ended, in order to make way for a new post-Protestant form of Christianity. In this time of change in her own life and in historical existence as a whole the church must strengthen her own life and must also transcend it. She strengthens herself by a deep and thorough union with that center of history which she proclaims and by which she lives. It is at the moment that she makes room for historical change that she needs the criterion by which all history is to be judged. The act of transcending herself is based upon the knowledge that there is an invisible history of the church, for which the visible churches are also responsible, and by which at the same time they are determined.

For the action of the church from within her own borders the special *kairos* of this period will consist in the preparation of a historical existence of her own after the self-destruction of the present structure of historical existence. This process of preparation includes three elements: being set free from entanglement with the disintegrating " demonic " forces of present history, fresh consideration of the ultimate criterion as compared with history as a whole, and the application of this criterion to ecclesiastical action both inside and outside the church.

(3) So far as the action of the church outside her own borders is concerned the present menace to historical existence summons her to represent the unity of the Kingdom of God in face of the divisions caused by the " demonic " forces. Where capitalism is concerned this means the application of the criterion of material justice. Where nationalism is concerned it means the application of the criterion of the unity of the human race. Where dictatorship is concerned it means the application of the criterion of the finite character, and yet at the same time the dignity of every human being.

The application of the criterion of justice to the present social situation means the destruction of the capitalistic class contrast and of the autonomous supremacy of economics over life as a whole. The use of the word " socialism " to describe this process does not mean a decision for a special party, but it does mean the concrete character of the demand for justice in the historical situation of disintegrating capitalism.

The application of the criterion of the unity of the human race to the present international situation means the removal of the dominating political sovereignty of the individual states. The use of the word " pacifism " for this demand does not mean the support of the present pacifist organizations, but the concrete character of the demand for peace in the historical situation of self-destructive nationalism.

The application of the criterion of the finite character and yet the dignity of every human being to the present political situation means the introduction of anti-dictatorial corrections into the structure of government. The use of the expression " the rights of man " for this demand does not mean the support of a liberalistic structure of society, but the concrete character of the Christian-humanistic demand, in a situation in which tyranny dominates the masses.

(4) It is in accordance with the idea of the *kairos* that that which the ultimate criterion requires is a promise and therefore an object of hope. And since, from the point of view of history, every promise is connected with the condition of human free activity, the hope of any historical realization remains doubtful. The only unconditional prospect is the promise and expectation of the supra-historical fulfilment of history, of the Kingdom of God, in which that which has not been decided within history will be decided and that which has not been fulfilled within history will be fulfilled.

The phenomenon which is described in the New Testament as interpretation of the " signs of the times " — the judgment on the " tendencies " of the present which is always presupposed in action — this signifies the unity of demand and expectation in interpreting history. In every period there are symptoms which show what is going on under the surface. The perception and the interpretation of these symptoms is the task of the prophetic spirit, which may appear either in a more intuitive or in a more rational form, but is never wholly without either the one or the other. The words of Jesus, " Repent, for the Kingdom of Heaven is at hand," represent in classic form that combination of demand and expectation which arises out of the interpretation of the *kairos*. The most magnificent theoretical interpretation and the most effective practical interpretation of an historical period was the Marxist analysis of capitalist society. It too united summons and demand with interpretation and expectation.

Historical interpretation from the point of view of the

kairos must resist the temptation to separate demand and expectation. Mere demand leads to pharisaism and moralistic utopianism. Just as the Jew who was loyal to the Law found it impossible to bring in the day of the Lord by force, so in our own day pacifists and utopian socialists have found it impossible to enforce world peace and social justice by means of moralistic propaganda. Only that which at least potentially exists as a reality can be realized historically. The Kingdom of God only comes at all because in Christ it is already " amongst us." World peace will only come in so far as the actual union of humanity has in principle removed the divisions caused by nationalism. The classless society will only come when the inward power of society has already been concentrated in *one* class. But all this does not imply any inevitable course of events. The Kingdom of God " tarries " in the process of drawing mankind together, new " confusions of tongues " break out, the class in which all classes are to be removed may fail, or may fall a prey to new divisions.

Neither prophetic promise nor historical dialectic speaks of things which *must* happen. It is not the prophet but the diviner, not the dialectician but the mechanist who tries to predict the course of history and thus tries to turn it into a natural process.

The certainty that these elements of demand and promise which a *kairos* contains will be fulfilled points to the supra-historical unity of the ultimate meaning. Here, and here only, all that is undecided in history is decided, and all that is unfulfilled is fulfilled. Therefore historical action can remain sure of itself, and the religious interpretation of history can defend its rights, even in face of the disappointment provided by unfulfilled expectation and fragmentary actualization. The question of history has a final answer: the Kingdom of God.

THE KINGDOM OF GOD AND
HISTORY

by

H. D. WENDLAND

THE KINGDOM OF GOD AND HISTORY

INTRODUCTION

THE work of the ecumenical research groups has of necessity raised the question of the Christian understanding of history, because it is concerned with the right action for the church in the world. For the church of Christ has a historical existence and must herself act continually in the world as part of the historical process. She administers the Word, trains and guides men, and lives through the historical process both within herself and in and with individuals and nations, indeed in and with all humanity. So she needs to be able to clarify and interpret contemporary historical decisions, since they affect her, and it is in their midst that she wishes to act, and, indeed, she must do so.

The Christian view of history is an eschatological one, interpreting history in the light of its coming and inevitable *end*. The attitude of the believing community therefore is one *of hope and expectation;* by this we mean a hope which is full of confidence, joy and a sense of victory in the eschatological sense. Thus the expectation of the end is more than a spirit of intense concentration on the future; it is rooted in God's saving deed in Christ in the past and the *present*. The specifically *Christian* view of history is, in this threefold sense, a *historical eschatology*. For it the eternal is neither purely present nor purely future. Its three main principles are the following:

1. God's Kingdom has come.
2. God's Kingdom is coming at the present time.
3. God's Kingdom will come.

This raises the following questions:

(*a*) What are we to understand by the Kingdom of God, and how is it revealed?

(*b*) How does the Kingdom of God enter into history?

(*c*) How are sacred and secular history interwoven?

(*d*) What is the end of history or the victory of God's Kingdom?

(*e*) What is the significance of the Christian view of history, with its message of the coming of God's Kingdom, for the church's situation and task in the world?

1. THE KINGDOM OF GOD [1]

(1) God's Kingdom is God's *sovereignty*, God's *basileuein*, i.e., his kingly rule.   God's sovereignty comes to the world, because he is the world's King and Lord, and it belongs to him alone.   God's Kingdom does not exist apart from his people; men are chosen for and called into his Kingdom.   God's Kingdom is a kingdom for the earth, for the whole of creation; it aims at becoming a kingdom on earth.   It is not a metaphysical realm behind or above this world, lying behind the things of this world or hovering over them.   *God comes;* that is the direct and simple import of the New Testament message of the Kingdom of God.

(2) God's Kingdom manifests itself as *judgment* and *salvation*. It lays bare every sin and summons to repentance.   It comes as forgiveness of sins and eternal life, already begun in this temporal order and consummated in the judgment and the new creation at the end of the days.

(3) God's Kingdom is transcendent and immanent, present and future alike.

(4) It is not possible to find any opposition between the

[1] (Cf. on this section W. Künneth: *Theologie der Auferstehung*, 2nd edition, 1934; H. D. Wendland, *Der Herr der Zeiten*, Cassel, 1936.)

trinitarian starting-point of Christian doctrine and that which is here chosen as the starting-point of the message of the Kingdom of God, namely, *eschatology*. For according to the witness of Holy Scripture this coming Kingdom of God manifests itself in threefold fashion:

It is the *Kingdom of the Father,* the *Kingdom of the Son,* and the *Kingdom of the Holy Ghost.*

Thus the eschatological gospel of the Kingdom is of necessity itself trinitarian in character.

2. THE ENTRANCE OF GOD'S KINGDOM INTO HISTORY

(1) God's Kingdom breaks into history (and in so doing itself becomes history) in the man Jesus of Nazareth, sent in the fulness of time as the mediator of God's sovereignty. In opposition to all theological definitions which would isolate one aspect or another of his work, we must emphasize the *totality* of this mission of his, by which God's Kingdom is brought into the world. In other words, we speak here neither only of the incarnation, nor only of the cross, nor only of the Redeemer's Spirit-filled words and deeds, but the acts of his mission are to be seen where they belong: in his mission as a whole.

When we think of Christ as " the center of history," this can only be true in virtue of his resurrection from the dead. This eschatological event having taken place in the midst of the history of this world, the latter takes on a new quality and points towards a new consummation. *He who has risen again is Lord of history, Lord of all times and all dimensions of historical reality in the past, the present, and the future.* As the *Risen One* Jesus is the *Lord who is to come again, judge of the world* in the glory of the Father, conqueror of all powers that set themselves against God, the *Victor* who sets up the Kingdom and hands it over to the Father.

So it is the resurrection, the turning-point of the aeons, which lies at the root of the Christian view of history; for without it the incarnation and the activity and death of the Lord within history are void of meaning. Without them we could not really speak of the Kingdom of God as coming.

God's Kingdom comes in Christ once for all as an actual event in history. It is this man Jesus, with his limitations in space and time. For only so can God's Kingdom come to men in their reality and historicity.

(2) Christ is the *center of history*. It is only because the Kingdom becomes history in Jesus Christ that history receives a center; previously it only contained the *promise* of that coming fulfilment.

(*a*) This idea of the " center of history " does not primarily distinguish between two historical epochs, as, for instance, in the case of the years 1914 and 1933. The distinction which it denotes is that between the old era of sin and death, and the new age of God and his salvation, which brings with it " life and blessedness." Christ is the turning-point for world history as a whole, including those epochs which are yet to come, and not those only which preceded the birth of Christ. Otherwise he would be merely a turning-point of the kind some historians and philosophers take him to be (as one outcome of the Christian influence at work in idealism, e.g., Fichte, Hegel, Ranke), but not the turning-point of world history as a whole, the sovereign Lord of all time.

All the same, the idea of a turning-point between two periods of history, as applied to Jesus, has a certain significance. For since the end of the world and its judgment have not yet arrived with his appearing, we live, from the Christian and eschatological point of view, in the interim period; thus, as a matter of fact, a new historical epoch did actually begin with Jesus, the special mark of which is the fact of the church, and the history of the church, in the midst of and interwoven with secular history. God having revealed himself as Three in One, the existence of the church is the deepest meaning of history, and even the solution of the problem of history as such. Such language is not the illusion of an orthodox absolutism, turning a blind eye to the sinful form in which the church appears. Nor is it ecclesiastical conservatism which regards the existence of the church as practically the fulfillment of history (Tillich). It is sober deduction from the eschatological gospel of the Kingdom; in and through the coming of God's sovereignty, through repentance and the forgiveness of sins the community of the last days, which waits till God's new world be made complete, comes into being.

Of course this interim period is to be distinguished from God's sovereignty when it is consummated, when sin, death and all the abominations of this world will have disappeared. And yet it is the " day of salvation " in which the gospel is proclaimed, the divine Spirit enlightens men's hearts and moves them to faith; it is the period of the history of the Christian church. To be sure, it is also the period in which unbelief opposes faith and saving history operates, secretly and paradoxically, under a history of Christianity and the church which is full of sin and apostasy from divine truth.

(b) To this sacred history, which is partly manifest and partly concealed, which begins with the mission of Jesus Christ, there belongs an equally paradoxical period of pre-history — the history of the preparation for and promise of salvation. Three events characterize it: (1) the *election of Israel* and the *conclusion of a covenant* between God and his people; (2) the *revelation of God's Law,* which his people is under obligation to keep; (3) the *prophetic promise* of the future messianic salvation and

the coming Kingdom, when peace and righteousness, forgiveness of sins, and the gift of the Spirit will prevail. In so
far as God's will here becomes law for a definite historical
people and God's community is represented outwardly in
this people, and in so far as God's will and its prophetic
servants meet with unbelief and disobedience, this pre-
historic period in the development of salvation is also
paradoxical, a rock of offense, veiled and hidden.

(c) Christ is the center of history; this principle affirms
further that Christ's claim is a *universal one,* a claim upon
all times, peoples, races and cultures. It is the claim to
be for them all the way, the truth and the life. Poor and
limited as the realization of this in the missionary enterprise
may be, the claim itself remains. Yes, it will always remain
limited and must be so, for Christ does not intend to make
his presence felt in this interim period with compelling,
external, absolutely overmastering power, but as one who
calls for decision, conversion, faith and discipleship, He
leaves to all tracts and times their freedom of decision, of
Yes and No. Yet when Christ is taken as the center of
history, this must needs be seen as a *unity and totality*. It
is from the Christian point of view alone that there is such
a thing as universal history, the history of humanity, and
not simply a confusion of a thousand factors and effects,
quite beyond our power to disentangle, nor simply the
juxtaposition of races or cultures with their periods of
growth and decay. History points to Christ and is derived
from him; the ages lead to him as their goal or take their
origin from him. The road from the creation to the day
when all shall be made complete runs through him, the
center and fulfilment of the ages; in him the earthly and
the heavenly become one.

(d) As Christ stands in the center of history, so also he
stands at the beginning and the end; he is the *Logos,* by

whom and in whom all that is was created. He is *judge* of
the world in the power of the Father. Because he is thus
the mediator of creation and the consummation, he can
be Lord of all ages, like God himself the beginning and
the end. Thus in *Christology,* the basis of a Christian
theology of history, it becomes clear that the foundation
of history, properly speaking, is twofold. In the first place,
there can be history only because there is creation, only
because there are creatures whom God created in the Logos
with God as their end, and endowed with the personal
qualities of spirit and will, and so with the capacity for
action, without which there can be no historical occur-
rence. For God has "determined the appointed seasons
for the nations of the earth, and the bounds of their habitation, that they should seek God" (Acts 17:26–27). For
the statement that man was created by the Logos and has
personal quality, that he was made in the image of God,
means this: that his being has God as its end, as a sign set
upon the creation to show the dignity of the Creator and
His right over him as His own. In the second place, there
can only be history *because there is sin.* "It is the fall
which furnished the presuppositions for the dynamic of the
historical process" (Tillich). "History is the concrete
form under which our *sarx* exists, and the *sarx* is the ground
and impulse of our historical character." [2] Thus the end
of history is the judgment and Christ is judge of the world.
The beginning of history is the existence of man as the
sinful creature in his will-to-be-himself. For this will is
only possible *because* he is a creation of God and so has life
and personality from him; at the same time it is only possible as he *turns away from* his creaturely status in *superbia,*
rebellion against the Creator and his commandment.

[2] Helmut Thielicke, *Geschichte und Existenz,* Gutersloh, 1935, p. 63.

3. SACRED HISTORY AND SECULAR HISTORY

(1) We have thought of our historical period as the interim period between the resurrection of Christ and the end of the world. From this the following conclusions are to be drawn:

(*a*) Sacred history means that through the mission of Christ, as this has been described above, God's salvation and grace are active in the world in the Holy Spirit, in the preaching of the Word, and in deeds of love. Salvation comes into the world, but the world as such is not yet full of salvation. But on the other hand sacred history is not some kind of supernatural causality which is inserted into the context of world history like another history by itself (historical supernaturalism). God's saving work is not something which one can point out and find ready to hand like other historical facts which occur; sacred history lies concealed in secular history under sin and death. Nevertheless it is real: (1) as a continually renewed presence of Christ in his community through the Word and the Spirit; (2) as a real historical continuity in the life of the church, with Christ as its source, as *successio fidei,* in which in faith we receive the gospel from our fathers and hand it on to future generations, so that out of this there grows the historical tradition of the church. Every time salvation becomes fact and every time the gospel is preached afresh it arouses the opposition of unbelief and of anti-Christian forces. Sacred history leads ever and again to the bearing of the cross.

(*b*) We must distinguish between sacred history and church history. For the church, as a community of sinful men in the midst of this world, also lives through a thoroughly secular history, full of illusion, guilt, the struggle for power, and all that is transitory. Thus although sacred history and church history can never coincide, the church, in spite of her own worldliness, remains the bearer of sacred history within secular history. In the church God's Kingdom is present in the Word, and with the Spirit, in sacraments and deeds of love. Hence sacred history can be sought and found only in the church; for she alone possesses the Word of God, and the sacraments as means of grace. The forces which carry on the process of secular history in their arrogance often look down on the church in her sorry " form of a slave," fully persuaded of the irresistible power which they possess — within the world! And yet they are outside sacred history and the actual center of history; they do not know God's saving decree. Rather it is of God's grace when men who are involved in secular history and are under the control of its forces, are reached by the gospel of salvation.

The relation of sacred and secular history is created by two things: by the proclamation of the message of salvation, and by faith — which makes man a member of the Body of Christ. Thus these two kinds of history are not simply closed to each other, and separate from one another. But this positive relation between the two is created by *the coming of the Kingdom,* and not by the fact that secular history itself contains any inherent sacredness, which is then merely fulfilled, completed, and perfected by sacred history. Since, however, God's Kingdom comes, and *becomes* history, not only does the judgment upon history begin (" Now is the prince of this world judged," John 12:31, 14:11), but also God's " Yes " to the historical process, which has in him its goal, begins to work: " That they should seek God." This " Yes " is judgment, freedom and redemption from the world and from the body of this death, but all by *love;* and the goal of this love is the making of a new and holy creation. The redemption *from* history

as death struggle, transitoriness and the distortion of all
life by demonic powers and egotism is at the same time the
consummation of history; it is as witness to this that sacred
history is present and active in, with, and behind secular
history.

(*c*) The *complete cancellation* of the contrast between
sacred and secular history lies in the future and is of a
purely eschatological character. The complete determination by the divine will of all created things (" God all in
all," 1 Cor. 15:28), brings to an end the dualism of sacred
and secular history which is a distinguishing feature of this
" interim period " of ours in which the two aeons are interwoven.

(*d*) *Then is the Kingdom of God realized in sacred history?* Yes, in so far as the coming of the Kingdom creates
and establishes a sacred history in this world.

No, in so far as the sovereignty of God will only be fully
established at the " end " of history, and sacred history,
because it is in the world, can never be wholly identical
with the divine sovereignty.

*Is God's Kingdom realized outside sacred history in secu-
lar history?* No doubt there are *Christian ages* and a *Christian world,* in which not only ideas and ethical values, but
also political and social developments, historical institutions, and certain forms of sovereignty can be seen to have
been permeated with Christian influences and to have received a Christian impression; so we speak of the medieval
" Christian empire," modern " Christian democracy," etc.
These are effects which arise when sacred history penetrates
into secular history. The world as society, culture, state
and nationality has in fact for centuries taken into itself
elements of the Christian message and Christian life. But
it has at the same time " absorbed " them, cutting them
loose from their native soil in sacred history and so ap-

prehending them as ideas in themselves, e.g., humanity, freedom, peace, justice, personality. Thus because every-thing of value has been absorbed by the world, the world forgets whence they came, and sacred history and the church seem to have become quite superfluous in the world; what they had to offer has been taken over, and what is left is a mere ruin, a rind from which everything has been squeezed out. The *Christian world* is a specious hybrid of sacred and secular history. For it is on the one hand an original and actual fact, historical reality, such as would be inconceivable apart from sacred history, as for example the whole spiritual, social and political history of the West to the present day. And yet the dissolution of Christianity arises in this sphere. For it always means *the secularization of the church; the more " Christian" the world, the more secular the church!* It is a matter of indifference whether this takes place in the form of a state church (the church as a department of the state for public worship) or in that of a religious association, a religious union on democratic soil, or in the form of the nation organized as a religious com-munity. "The Christian world" and the "realization of Christian ideals in society" simply *ends* in the radical secularization of the Christian world; the world says more clearly and with more emphasis what is said by a Chris-tianity which has entered the world and become embedded in it! The ground and origin of the Christian elements which remain unappropriated become less and less known; they pass out of sight. The Christian world ends once more in a world which can account for itself without introducing a single factor from outside, while the secularized church ends in Judaism or heathenism or a mixture of the two. For as heathenism and Judaism arise today in a *post-Christian world,* they begin by adapting to their purpose the figure and mission of Christ, but in the end they reveal their basic character as *anti-Christian religions* which worship man or nature or historical development or moral achievement.

In spite of all this, the effect of sacred history upon secular history is never destroyed, and the gates of hell do not swallow up the church. The victories which the world wins are Pyrrhic victories, preparing the way for its own overthrow, even when Christ and Antichrist, faith and unbelief stand out in the confusion of secular history increasingly clearly as the decisive antitheses.

(2) The *structure of secular history,* which we have hitherto kept separate from sacred history (yet not forgetting that both appear paradoxically intertwined in the history of Christianity and the church) is due to the truths which we have already mentioned, namely: that God is the Lord of history, and Christ the beginning, the middle and the end of history.

This means that the structure of history is due to *creatureliness and sin.*

Two extreme views are to be rejected:

(a) The *view of history which centers in the fact of sin,* for which history is seen as a single descending line, as a progressive fall into sin and advance towards judgment. In the last resort this view casts a doubt upon the presence of God as creator and sovereign. Such a view of history, strictly speaking, can only be maintained with the aid of a gnostic type of thinking and an absolutely dualistic idea of the world, so that the world, conceived as the work of an evil deity, is opposed to the strange, unknown and wholly transcendent God of redemption.

(b) The *natural theology of history,* nourished on the Enlightenment and idealism and summed up in the confession: God is *in* history. Connected with it are the thought of an ascending unfolding or development within history (progress towards the final goal of a perfected condition of the world, but with this conceived as a historical period) , and the notion that we men who know and experience history, in the divine meaning of the historical process possess a datum, be it rational or irrational in character, which is immediately and directly accessible.

Now in virtue of our faith in God as creator and Lord we who hold the Christian view of history are also familiar with the thought of the *guidance and direction* of history by God, and the thought of a divine Providence which overrules the confusion of secular history. But these ideas are to be understood eschatologically; that is to say, the goal and the end is the coming salvation and the new creation. All God's action in the history of the *world,* as the one who created, rules, and upholds it, has a secret and invisible, one might almost say a subterranean connection with the creation of *God's people* and the establishment of *God's Kingdom* (this is the message of Old Testament prophecy) . Whatever the Lord of history may do serves his plan of redemption, incomprehensible though this must often appear to us, when we fix our eyes on the calamity and destruction, shame and disgrace, horror and disaster, on all the demonic powers which are let loose in world history.

What then is it which causes God's sovereignty in world history to be hidden?

The answer contains two points of view, which again can be summed up in a single phrase: by the fact that the structure of this world is one of *sin and death.*

(*a*) This is to be seen first of all in man and in human associations, as man's autocratic self-will, wanting to rule by itself and alone. The human world wants to live that life which was given to it in creation as its own without God, and, indeed, in opposition to him. This is the origin of the distortion of our life as God's creation and the deep-

seated malady which afflicts us; we constantly claim as our
own achievement what we have received as a gift, and so
set ourselves up as gods and demiurges. *Amor sui*, self-
love, permeates all action in the realm of history. How
could history exist were it not for the terrific driving-power
of the will-to-live, by which individuals and great societies
alike each want to live their own life, to maintain, enhance,
establish and expand this life? Are not even these societies
always full of " collective self-assertion "? The whole of
history is a fallen creation and at every moment it is falling
afresh! [3] The whole of history is in need of redemption;
all the great developments of history, institutions, states,
nations, make themselves and their maintenance the object of their wills and make autonomy and self-government
their aim. The conflicts within history between states,
nations, estates, classes and generations are brought about
by collisions between various bodies animated by the will
to live and the will to be different from others. Self-
assertion, competition and oppression are written across the
ambiguous countenance of world history.

(*b*) Yet this aspect of will in men and human societies
is a phenomenon with far deeper roots. It is as if there
were *total laws, objective forces and powers* — independent of man, and yet ruling him and holding him captive —
at work in history: the principalities and powers of this
world, ultimately *one* in the kingdom of the *prince or god
of this age*. Paul speaks not only of sins, but also of sin as a
power which invests, lays claim to, and permeates with its
authority the whole world and all human existence. In this
polarity of objective and subjective, the kingdom of Satan
and my sin, lies the strange secret of evil. It is a force and a
sovereignty *over us*, a power which governs history — and
yet it is my will and my passion. These powers are typical

---

[3] Cf. H. Thielicke, *Geschichte und Existenz*, pp. 18, 38 ff., 63.

of the world, as they live on their own resources, making themselves their aim and wanting to govern themselves, as a will opposed to God. It is they who conceal the presence of God in world history, who spread darkness and lies, who pervert the creation and create the illusion that what is in the world is autonomous, because they show man and the world in seductive brilliance as themselves divine.

(c) *Yet the kingdom of Satan is never to be equated simply with secular history.* In spite of all his power to introduce confusion, he never succeeds in nullifying the fact that the world is God's creation and in snatching it out of his hands. Nor may God's Kingdom and Satan's ever be regarded merely as counterparts on the same level. For in the first place, concealed as it is, God's Kingdom is always the victor; and in the second, the world remains God's creation, and the demonic element in it is always a perversion of a life which neither the demons nor Satan created. Although it is certain that this demonic power can assume historical form, we must be on our guard against naïvely regarding a given historical phenomenon as the demonic kingdom, for this leads to an all-too-simple presentation of history as a sketch in black and white; as, for example, when the operation of demonic forces is regarded as incorporated in capitalism alone, or in Bolshevism alone, or in the political power, the state as such. The consequence of such a view in the Christian community is pharisaism or fanaticism, for it then thinks of itself as spotless and holy, and the *simul justus simul peccator* is ignored. The activity of Antichrist is possible everywhere: no doubt, he appears in a historical form, but he is not simply identical with it, nor is he confined to this one form. Especially the power of evil must be regarded as a force which rules and enslaves man and humanity *as a whole.* Even the Apocalypse does not discern the presence of Antichrist only in the power of

Rome, deifying itself in the worship of the emperor, but also in Judaism as "the synagogue of Satan," and in anti-Christian movements within the church.

(d) If we reject a theology which finds in sin and the power of death the sole criteria for the interpretation of secular history, we are also in the position to reach a positive understanding of the *historical work of humanity* in the creation of states and civilizations, in the widest sense of those terms.

God gave man freedom and the power to create. God has never revoked this creative act. He has given man sovereignty over the earth and the rest of creation. It is in his possession of this independence and power that man shows on his forehead the mark of honor set there by God, which singles him out as the handiwork of such a creator. It is God's will that man should create and achieve. He himself works in concealment, using men's actions and decisions. Man's deeds are a work wrought in him by Another and are the creation of the Creator: they arise out of gifts and powers which have been bestowed upon him. Thus a perception of the demonic character of self-assertion does not finally solve the problem of the extent to which human and historical actions are autonomous. There is a God-appointed *obligation* to *earthly* labor, though this again does not obscure the sharp line of demarcation between the Kingdom of God and secular history. To be sure, to work in history under the mandate of and with the powers given by the Creator is not to set up the Kingdom of God. Yet the fact remains that God wants us to work with him, and that " He does us the honor of wanting to work his work with us and through us." [4] What has been said of man's power to modify and create does not invalidate what was said of the demonic element

4 Luther: WA 6, 227.

in history. That man is sexually determined, that he has power to form projects and to carry them out — this his endowment as a creature becomes a temptation to him when he ascribes it to himself alone, instead of serving God in it and with it and doing all his historical work to the glory of God, since he wishes to be praised in the conduct of his creatures. So arise the demonic forces of sexuality and power and many others; we turn the honor which God does to us into our own honor. From this arises the profound ambiguity of all historical work. But for all that, to the end of history, God does not cease to do his work through men, both through those who do his will as well as through those who perforce serve him against their will as instruments. This is why history always seems to arise simply out of the collaboration of a number of human wills.

Since, in spite of man's sinfulness, God has given him an obligation to earthly labor, he has made him steward of those goods and forms of association without which human action in history would be inconceivable. Man engages in economic activities; he builds states; he creates the values of culture; in marriage and the family he propagates the life the Creator gave him. God makes history a realm of objective development and appoints man as its steward. This involves two things:

1. The *independence* which God gave him when he handed over and entrusted to him these goods and social institutions;

2. The *responsibility* of all historical action in the presence of *the Judge of all,* the secret reference of every historical event to the coming judgment. The steward is not the Lord; the Lord is as yet far away, but he is coming to hold a reckoning with the stewards of his property.

Because the goal of the whole of God's creation is the

future new creation, the wealth of historical acts and deeds, as well as the social forms in which they are accomplished, means that they are not merely instruments of sacred history and the final selection of the completed people of God; they have their own hidden eschatological meaning. We must avoid bringing sacred and secular history into relation to each other by some " pietistic " scheme which allows the whole of secular history to evaporate into something indifferent, and sees in the formation of the community of Jesus the *sole* meaning of *every* event in secular history; we must also avoid the mistake of raising secular history itself to the level of sacred history in certain events or achievements. Sacred and secular history have a *single* goal in God's new creation; secular history goes forward to the judgment. The Christian church cannot anticipate this judgment, especially as it must itself appear before the judgment seat of Christ.

(*e*) Does the historical labor of humanity give any signs of *progress?* We agree here with Tillich that there is technical and scientific progress, and progress in the art of civilization, and even to a very great extent; but this may be accompanied by cultural degeneration. From the theological point of view it is of the utmost importance to note that each advance in man's rule of the world brings with it a fresh form of the demonic; thus the age of modern science brings the demonic in the form of a denial of God on grounds of reason; the age of technical improvement, the degradation of man to a slave or to a function within a system of machine-production; the capitalistic intoxication of an absolutely limitless expansion of production and profit produces the worship of mammon; the conquest of space and time by radio and air transport, man's enslavement to speed and an imperialistic desire to expand. Each advance has its own form of the demonic. This indicates that man is not able to break through the framework of human history in the *sarx* by all his progress and that it does not belong to the Kingdom of God. A further question is that of moral progress in history. Certainly as in the life of the individual so also in the conditions which obtain within whole human groups and ages there are certain ethical heights and depths; but we cannot speak of a continuous ethical progress in the sense of an ascending development. There is as little place for the righteousness of " works " in the Christian doctrine of history as in soteriology in the stricter sense. For if there is ethical progress, it must consist of a conquest of evil. Those who think of evil as something in the nature of an imperfection may believe that they can observe something of that kind. But those who know that evil is a positive power arrayed against the divine, see that it has not yet been overcome by moral progress (of the natural man, thinking and willing " ethically "), and can never be so overcome. There is no ethical process which leads from earth to heaven. The New Testament sees the most frightful concentration of satanic power take place just before the end. That is a proof that the sign that God's sovereignty is at hand is not progress, but a sharp distinction between faith and unbelief, Christ and Antichrist, the church and the world.

True progress in world history lies rather, quite simply, in the fact that *sacred history* has entered into secular history, and thus that such things as a life in Christ, faith, love and sanctification actually exist. But all this remains within this aeon which is in conflict with the principalities and powers of this world, although, on the other hand, in Christ we know that the process of " dying to the world and to sin " has begun. Thus it is not to be denied that there are Christians who *increase and grow in sanctification;* but these very people are aware that their sanctifica-

tion is God's work in them, and that their condition remains one of struggle, because so long as we are in this
life " a tiny spark of flesh cleaves to us " (Luther) all the
time. This knowledge does not mean resignation. For
in Christ we have received warning and promise for the
struggle for sanctification. Growth in Christ is of course
never an advance in a straight line, for it is just because we
are being sanctified that we are constantly led to repentance, so that it can be said: " God lets us advance as dying
men." [5] This alone can be called *Christian* progress, due
to the entrance of salvation into secular history.

4. THE VICTORY OF GOD'S KINGDOM AND THE END OF HISTORY

(1) World history is not the judgment, but is proceed-
ing towards the judgment. God's judgment in history, in
the downfall of peoples and empires, in the visitation of
whole churches, in chastisement, foreshadows the last judgment. This judgment is the *end of* history. God's Kingdom cannot be finally completed without judgment, since
it comes to a history full of sin and death. The judgment
shatters and destroys secular history with its structure of
sin and death; that kind of history which in all its positive
development is also always " passing away," involving in its
destruction everything that takes place, so that nothing can
remain intact, not even the church of Christ in its earthly
form and organization. For if when God's people have
been perfected, the Christian seer gazing into the future
exclaims: " I saw no temple therein," because God himself dwells in the midst of his redeemed people, this means:
(1) that the *dualism of* sacred and secular history will be
transcended, and also (2) that the church will *be freed
from the form in which* it has passed through a " church

[5] Thielicke, op. cit., p. 259.

history " of a very earthly character, a prey to division, error and sin.   At this point the important thing is to hold fast the realism of the New Testament promise.   World history will have a *real* end, whatever antinomies for thought may be forced on us by such a message, because our thinking, in bondage as it is to time and history, cannot conceive of such an " end."   The " end " is therefore by no means merely a " symbolical " expression for the transcendent meaning of our existence.   If the framework of history has as it were been broken and shattered by the incarnation and resurrection of Christ, it will come to an end and be done away with in and at his fresh coming to the world. To make the " end " of history a symbol of transcendence would logically involve the same process with the concrete act by which the Word was made flesh.   And that which the world — in opposition to the Christian conviction of the end — calls " infinity " and " eternity " in the light of God's Kingdom is seen to be merely finite.   From the face of God heaven and earth flee away (Rev. 20:11).   The parousia of the Lord is the end of history and of this age at a particular time and hour, towards which the world's history tends.   At the same time of course the parousia completely shatters the form of this world and the structure of secular history; and in so far as it does this it is " beyond " time and history.   We must, therefore, think of the end of history neither " idealistically " as a timeless eternity which abides above the world, nor as a purely temporal event within the historical process; in neither case could we speak of the last judgment or of the end of history.   This end of history is *redemption from history in the sarx;* for in God's new world there is neither mourning nor crying, nor pain, nor tears any more, for the first things are passed away.

(2)   Behold! all things have become new: a *new creation*

full of *eternal life*.   For the problem of history this means the consummation of all development, the fulfilment of every living thing in creation, man's labor in history and his life in time and history as well, since by these God has called us to action.   God's new world is eternal *life,* not death, not absolute rest, not annihilation.   And in the same way God's Kingdom is the consummation of history, a consummation wrought by God through the power of Christ, and not through progressive self-unfolding and enhancement.   But it is at the same time the consummation of *God's creation* where it did not fall from him; God's Kingdom is *the telos of all history,* not of sacred history alone.

(3) This indicates at the outset what answer is to be given to the question of *the outcome of history.*

On the one hand the New Testament says that the outcome of history is the separation of the " children of the Kingdom " from the " children of the evil one." [6]   But on the other hand it speaks of the kings of the earth bringing their glory into the heavenly Jerusalem and the nations walking in its light.[7]   Is the outcome of history to be found therefore only in the church of the redeemed?   No doubt this is the center of God's new world; for it gathers up all the glory of earth, and henceforth its light fills the whole new world.   But on the other hand it is equally true to say that the perfecting of the church implies a new *world.*   The complete elimination of the secular is not the object of Christian hope but the doctrine of mysticism.   That God shall be " all in all " does not mean that the All will be dissolved in God and lost in him, but that everything will be filled and permeated with God's sovereignty, will and salvation.   If, however, the divine consummation reaches beyond the Christian community and means a new crea-

[6] Cf. Matt. 13: 24 ff., 38, and also Thielicke, op. cit., p. 328.
[7] Rev. 21:24, 26; cf. Isa. 60.

tion, if we have spoken of the consummation of the historical process, this means that, as a matter of fact, there is an actual outcome to history. We cannot demarcate and define it in detail; even that which to us seems meaningless, and even the demonic, must serve God's purposes. But in any case secular history is no mere means to the creation of God's redeemed community, it is and remains, in spite of sin and death, the development and the life of a divine creation. Here, too, it is true to say that God's Kingdom is his " Yes " to creation.

There is *no* outcome of history as such, and in so far as it is *in opposition to God*. In this case the sole outcome is the negative one of sin and death.

But the outcome of history in the positive sense is the goal to which God leads his creatures along the path of world history, and all that in his secret will he considers worthy to serve the final establishment of his Kingdom. The value of the historical labors of humanity from the point of view of the divine purpose is the secret of the divine judgment.

(4) There are, however, other contemporary views of history for which a picture of the final goal and the final condition of history is decisive, and they also have an idea of the outcome and goal of history. We call them *secular messianisms* or *utopias*. As regards their formal structure they seem closely akin to the Christian view of history; nor is this appearance deceptive, in so far as these utopias have been profoundly influenced by the Christian expectation of the Kingdom of God as the consummation of history, although this has been perverted and recast by them. These views may be summed up as follows:

(a) the *liberal and humanitarian* views;
(b) the *Marxist* view;
(c) the *nationalistic* utopias.

On German soil the idealistic philosophy of history (Kant,

Schiller, Fichte) exercised great influence on the formation of these various types of utopia; for them the goal
of history is a kingdom of absolute spirit, in which the
cultural improvement and creative self-development of
humanity has advanced to a condition of completion and
finality. This philosophical picture of the future with its
strong tinge of aestheticism [8] no longer wields any power
as a whole, but individual elements of it have entered into
the above-mentioned utopias, the peculiar feature of which
is that they take their stand on a *concrete political* decision
for democracy! For the workers of the world! For the
Nordic race!

The basic structure common to these secular forms of
messianism is evident in the following points:

(1) In the way in which the eschatological sovereignty
of God is reduced to something secular and finite. This
no longer remains the point at which history breaks off
and comes to an end, but is transformed into a goal within
history and a final condition of history, which again is
part of the historical process. It is a redemption in history,
but not at the same time a redemption from history, as in
the Christian expectation of God's Kingdom. The final
goal is either the *democratic society* of liberty, equality and
fraternity, prosperity and peace, or the *classless society* in
which the aim is an equal share for each in all goods, or a
political organization of the world as crown of the time
process and with a metaphysical halo, as in the idea of a
kingdom (Reich), or in that of " the elect nation " which
as the " Christophorus " or the " God-bearer " (the messianism of Russian Christianity) has received a special
vocation to the leadership of a particular epoch in history
or of humanity in general. Here the very terms which are
employed show clearly the connection of such a view with

---

[8] Cf. Fichte on the " Kingdom of Reason and Art."

Christian eschatology and the Christian view of history. The last-named messianism, with its reference to a nation or a kingdom, is to be met with in Russia and England as well as in France and Germany. It has often been connected with the democratic utopia, with its talk of " the nation which arises to lead humanity to true democracy and culture." The creation of this temporal kingdom rests either with some anonymous process of development or with man's own power to modify circumstances. This final kingdom is no longer really conceived as one which comes from God and by his power; if, however, God is mentioned, it is the God in man or the God who shows favor to a particular human group and whose help that group may claim; the " German " God, for example, is he " who blesses *us* and will give *us* the victory."

(2) In the rejection of Christ, which is the basic decision implicit in all these profane messianisms. What we have in them is a messianism without a messiah, that is to say without the true Messiah; in his place appear man or historical progress or " reason " or " spirit." Of course, all these substitutes are interconnected; all that happens is that the emphasis is distributed differently in each instance. In any case the Christian hope is exploited for secular ends; what is decisive for and central to the Christian expectation and view of history is forcibly removed. For in place of the expectation of the Christ of God, the " Adam of the last days," we have a general expectation of some final kingdom, and sacred history is accordingly dissolved in secular history, while secular history in its turn is directly or indirectly turned into sacred history.

(3) As, however, the coming of the final Kingdom cannot be thought of without those who bear authority in it, either the proletariat (Marxism) , or a kingdom, a nation (nationalist utopias) , or civil society (democracy and

liberalism) , steps into the place which has been left empty
at the center of the Christian hope and acts as substitute
for it.   Once again the *Kingdom of God* is turned into the
kingdom of man, of humanity, and man wants to redeem
and perfect the world by *his* sovereignty.

(4)   This brings us to the attitude of secular messianisms
to the church.   Either (*a*) the coming final Kingdom
makes the church superfluous and absorbs it into itself;
an expectation of this kind results in indifference to the
present day or to the attempt to draw the church as an
instrument into the political and social movement which
aims at the final kingdom; or (*b*) the coming final Kingdom, because it is conceived as a kingdom of man, *annihi-
lates* the church; it engages in a systematic campaign against
it and sets up an opposition church of a political and social
character which claims to be the new redeemed community.

(5)   The qualitative opposition of *God's Kingdom and
the power of Satan* is *altered;* evil is either denied outright
or transformed into a mere negative, an imperfection or a
hindrance to development (so that it can in the end become a necessary stage in progress) , or, in the third place,
it is concentrated in a particular historical phenomenon,
such as the capitalist class, dictatorship, nationalism, with
which, then, the suffering, innocent, pure, just persons
are contrasted.

(6)   These pseudo-messianic expectations cannot be
eliminated by means of theological criticism alone.   For
there is something further, something true and genuine
at work in them, which Satan, to be sure, seeks to use for
his own ends.   This is the recollection of Paradise which
remains impressed on the human mind, and man's knowledge that his goal is in the future; as God's creation he is
related both to the beginning and to the end of history.

This false faith in utopias springs out of the passionate longing in man, which nothing can stifle, for a *new creation*, a *restoration of human nature*. He can neither live nor think without the quest for completion and perfection. Would that man could understand this! For in his very faith in these utopias man bears witness against himself that he has sinned and fallen away from God. Yes! a new world and a new human race will come and must come; that is the deep and abiding truth in all utopias. But the one who alone can renew the world, through whom a new humanity can come into being, is Jesus Christ. Secular messianism will not accept this, and ends in the delusion of self-redemption. That means to decide for Antichrist; for the fulfilment of time, the guarantee of the consummation of God's Kingdom, *has* come to pass; they who believe in these utopias want to seize for themselves what God has given, which brings with it the certainty of the desired consummation. They set up a counter-hope, and thus declare themselves on the side of Antichrist.

Thus secular messianism is a tangle of man's genuine yearning for redemption and his will to assert his sovereignty against God. In this situation we ought to hear the challenge of need and of hope, and at the same time to ask ourselves whether the *church* has not been unfaithful to its task.

In point of fact to some extent the church is to blame for the appearance of this faith in utopias. For in its preaching of the Christian message there are two elements which it has almost ceased to proclaim: the *universalism* and the *realism* of the gospel of God's future sovereignty, which affirm that God's Kingdom will embrace the whole world and will be a new earth full of the enhancement of all the " creaturely " and human side of life. Instead of this it has surrendered (at least in continental Protestant theology) to a " spiritual " piety and to individualism. " Religious Socialism " was right to object to this, and in the same way these social and political utopias are right in their criticism of the church, in so far as they are a passionate protest against an individualistic piety whose sole concern is with the next world, which no longer has any universal hope for this world, but renounces history as a whole and has nothing left except a hope of salvation for the individual soul.

Confronted by these weaknesses and failures on the part of the church's preaching and attitude there is only one thing to do. We must struggle for a fresh proclamation of the genuine and complete eschatology of the sovereignty of God, as this came into the world through Jesus Christ, and will be consummated by him, bringing with it a new creation and a new and redeemed humanity which lives in the presence of God.

The realism of this gospel is the one positive answer to the question of the coming of the consummation of all things as this is asked so passionately by those who believe in these utopias. The preaching of the coming of God, who as King and Lord of the world will be and is its sole consummator and redeemer, is the most drastic *criticism* of these utopias.

(7) It is evident that when nowadays the relation of Christianity to the modern state is discussed, *national messianism* is the center of the discussion. It is intelligible that a phenomenon like German National Socialism, or Italian fascism, or the Japanese national revival, which derives its vitality from a religious consciousness of a national mission, and plays an extremely active part in contemporary history, should excite the keenest discussion. But we must call attention to the fact that at the outset *national messianism* was closely bound *up with the ori-*

gin of the modern Western nation-state, and that without it these states would not have been what they are today, for good as well as for evil. This fact once established, it is no longer possible with pharisaic indignation and superiority to lay the charge of national messianism at the door of certain nations, as particularly abominable instances of the demonic. It is not the case that where, for example, the idea of democracy is a living one, no national messianism did or could prevail. Rather there is a close connection between the two, as when a particular nation feels itself charged with a democratic mission to mankind. A national vocation and an aim of a universal character for mankind — these two have constantly been fused together in the Western nations. The consciousness of a national vocation on behalf of mankind, or even of the Kingdom of God, contributed as much as anything to give the European nations their present sharply defined characteristics and to make possible their extraordinary achievements, in the course of history, through which they have established white supremacy over mankind. National messianism is, therefore, neither a new (purely post-war) phenomenon, nor can it be ascribed to particular nations. When we speak of it, we must take into account the history and the present position, the greatness and the guilt of the European nations in general.

Since the collapse of the unified society of the Middle Ages under pope and emperor, dominated by the church, the following elements have been associated in national messianism:

(a) The national consciousness struggling to emerge from this unified society;

(b) The thought that for each individual nation there is a *special historical task* and vocation. " No imperialism could develop without such a consciousness of worth or vocation. The nationalism of the Western nations is in every case associated with a particular consciousness of vocation " (Tillich) ;

(c) This consciousness of vocation had a twofold Christian basis:

(i) in the faith in the *Creator and Lord* of the realm of history, who has given this nation its specific quality and gifts and in so doing also calls it to his service;

(ii) in the faith in *God's Kingdom,* by which the nations and their rulers are called to protect and further the establishment of God's Kingdom and the preaching of the gospel.

(d) This consciousness of vocation associates the nation with a *universal goal* for world history, so that the individual nation is thought of as one through which this final aim is to be realized.

(e) The national consciousness of vocation falls a prey to the general *process of secularization*; it loses its character of obedience to and service of a task received from God, before whom the people he has called still remain sinners, an instrument which he can reject. There then arises the idea of a *messianic kingdom* or *people* which leads in the end to the worship of individual nations as though they were idols, when all the restraints of Christian faith have been broken down. What was originally a religious imperialism, governed by the will to strive for the final kingdom, becomes a purely profane, political and economic will-to-power and will-to-exploit, which in the end dispenses with its religious garb altogether, and in this degenerate form becomes a sham which the white man imposes on the colored peoples, though it does not deceive them. Or, instead of God's Kingdom as the basis, humanity, culture, or a new human society in which peace prevails are set up as ideals at which to aim.

But a clear distinction should be drawn between a national messianism of this kind and the knowledge, which *Christianity is prepared to sanction,* that a nation receives its life and specific quality as gifts of the divine Creator, and just as the peculiar and personal existence of an individual human being is a divine gift, so also the nation has been given a *responsibility and a task* which it must seek to know and to fulfil. But those who have this sense of vocation must never forget that they are *instruments* only. At any time a nation may lose its high position and its rank in the order of history by the judgment of God. To none is eternity guaranteed and none can make itself eternal as a nation. Yet while criticism of religious nationalism is justified, we have no right to dismiss with contempt *every effort after a Christian understanding of a national reality and a national task.*

Although we must reject emphatically every form of national paganism and messianism, the true concern of nationalism must certainly be accepted. The Christian task is not discharged simply by criticism and rejection.

And so along with what was said above of the nation as a divine gift of the Creator, we must now turn to the problem of the *vocation of nations in the history of the world.* At this point we must distinguish three different situations and ideas:

(1) God entrusts each nation with a different historical task, different in its position in space and time, in its greatness and the duration of its life. Here we are thinking of a call from the Creator and Lord of history *within the historical process,* and to historical action. These vocations are subject to *temporal limitations.* We need to retain the stern thought of Luther, which he learned mainly from the Old Testament: that God may shatter and reject the instruments which he has employed.

Greece, Rome, and the universal empire of the Middle Ages were among those which had such vocations. God exalts kingdoms and nations, gives them glory and power, great leaders and great thinkers, but when it pleases him, he brings to nought all this earthly splendor, which is, indeed, his gift. His wisdom and power work in secret behind the rise and fall of world empires and their heroes; in the very fact that he thus elects and disposes of men and nations within the course of history, he is the *God who hides himself*. A vocation of this kind within the historical process *may* find its expression in the consciousness — on the part of empires and nations — of a definite historical vocation, as in Rome and in the medieval imperium, but it is not *bound* to do so. Such a *consciousness* of vocation is in danger of degeneration unless the Christian message of repentance and judgment defines its limits.[9]

(2) We must distinguish clearly between this kind of historical vocation and that *vocation to the Kingdom of God* which comes in the preaching of the gospel to all nations. This is the origin of the church of Christ in all nations, and she alone has the right to call herself *God's people* — on the ground of the divine call to salvation. This people of God or church is the end of, and exercises a criticism upon every national messianism and every attempt of the nation to set itself up in the place of God. Inasmuch as Jesus Christ has come and by his mission has brought into existence the true people of God, the equation of an imperial people belonging to nature and history with the people of God has been done away with and made impossible. This applied to Israel as well, for the saying: "We are Abraham's children" no longer carries with it any guarantee of salvation. The judgment falls on Israel, and the same repentance is required of him as of all those

---

[9] Cf. para. (3) below.

who want to become Christians from among the Ethnē,
the heathen nations. But if it is the case with regard to
" Israel after the flesh " that Christ is the end of the old
method by which God's people was embodied in a community belonging to nature and history, how much more
is this the case with those nations which never stood, as
Israel did, under the promise of salvation! In the Christian era there is no substitute for Israel; the people of
God is *in* all nations and is called *out of* all nations into *one
new body,* a new humanity (Eph. 2: 11f.). But of course
the creation of this new people of God no more annuls the
efficacy of particular vocations within the course of history
than it does the natural peculiarities of the nations (Holy
Scripture is translated!). The church is then differentiated according to nations, but this is the way in which the
Body of Christ is made flesh; it is not an organization of
religion in national churches serving national interests.

(3) But we have not finished with our question when
we have drawn a distinction between these two vocations.
The medieval idea of a Christian empire and the consciousness of a mission which we find in the nations of the
modern world alike draw our attention to a further state
of things: there are *vocations* within the historical process
and addressed to particular nations, or it may be to a
group of nations, *in relation to the church of Christ and
its task in the world.* So various nations become aware
that they are called as *whole entities to the service of
Christ and his church.* That is how I understand
the original Christian form of the Anglo-Saxon consciousness of a mission. To this corresponds the notion
which constantly meets us in the theology and historical
literature of continental Protestantism, that with the puri-
fying of the church by the reformed preaching of the gospel there has been given, for example, to the German na-

tion from God a historical task of service for the true
church of Christ, a task which it cannot with impunity repudiate, for if it does so it will incur God's judgment.
This notion is only possible if we begin with the assumption that the nations are represented in the great individuals whom God calls, and that these again have a God-
appointed task to carry out for their nations.   Thus the
German Reformation is regarded as a manifestation of
God's grace to the German people, but in no exclusive
sense, for the same truth was given by God to other nations
through Luther.   In this way such a task brings the *German* Reformation into association with the *whole church,*
and with many *other nations.*   Thus the vocation to
Christian service which comes within history to a particular people broadens out into a realm with suprana-
tional reference; it is related to ecumenical Christianity.
At the same time it is akin to the type of vocation which
belongs merely to secular history because it can be lost
(God's Word is like a passing shower).   It cannot be taken
for granted that the Germans will remain the " people of
the Reformation "; we might show ourselves to be un-
worthy of the call and commission which came to us.   The
same thing applies to every other nation within Christendom.   Not only does a responsibility on the part of the individual member of the nation follow from such a vocation
to the service of the church and the gospel within history,
but also a responsibility on the part of the organized public
life of the nation and the state, particularly on the part of
its leader — in relation to Christianity and the church.
Certainly not in the sense that the secular and political
organization may take upon itself ecclesiastical functions
nor in the sense that it should subject itself to ecclesiastical
sovereignty, but in the sense that it should respect and protect the church and should leave it a free sphere in which

to exercise its whole activity. And although it is certainly the case that *faith* can be aroused only by the *church's* preaching, still the nation as a whole has been called into the service of the divine mandate which was given to it with the Reformation, and its refusal would mean disobedience and judgment.

This notion of a limited vocation of nations within history to serve the growth and increase of Christianity rests upon a fact which *no unbelief can ever expunge* from the history of the West, that it is *only through and with the Christian gospel that the Western nations have come to themselves and become historical unities.*

The line of demarcation between the consciousness of a nation that it is called to such a task and the seduction of national messianism is narrow and thin. The distinction is that between knowing oneself to be but an *instrument,* and therefore being *prepared to repent,* and the *hybris* which misses what is laid up for it in eternity in order to secure the exaltation of its own people. Knowing oneself to be an instrument in the hands of God is something quite different from the will to world domination and the illusion of world redemption by means of men, classes, or nations. This will and this illusion are demonic in character. On the other hand it is a *Christian duty* to ask what God's will is for my people, the service allotted to it in the world and in relation to Christianity, though when we ask such questions we must be content to grope for an answer and to risk error. Messianism is a denial of God's judgment, while the consciousness of oneself as an instrument carries with it submission to God's judgment, because it sees that the nations are dependent on the will of God. It knows nothing of a mission which is guaranteed and exempt from change. This consciousness that one is an instrument in the hands of God can only arise

where the influence of the Christian church is a vital one
and permeates the nations. It is distinguished from the
knowledge of the general creaturely status of man and nation by its inclusion of the will to an historical task and an
historical goal.

5. HOW FAR CAN WE KNOW GOD'S OPERATION IN HISTORY?

(1) What man is, he is in history; I am my history, my
time. The whole man is historical, in body, soul, and
spirit.

(2) Because man is historical existence, he raises the
question of the meaning of history. Historical existence
has three characteristics: (a) as *recollection,* as reference
to and therefore also consciousness of past events, (b) as
demand arising out of the present, in which decision and
action are called for, (c) as *direction towards the future*
and what has not yet come to pass, therefore as an expectation, in which, however, man also attempts, both as an individual and as a nation, to determine his future and to
solve its riddle.

(3) The problem of *transcendence in history* arises in
the case of each of the three dimensions of historical existence. It is the historical character of human life itself
which evokes the question of the " divine " in the quite
general and indefinite sense of a *Higher Power* which we
encounter and by which we are determined. Man seeks to
find the *names* by which to conjure the abysmal, undis-
closed depths of history. Even the most rational attempts
to determine the laws of forces which direct and determine
history are but secularizations of the original and religious
attempt to approach the secret of history.

(4) A merely rational knowledge of history is not able
to answer the question of the meaning and goal of history.

As, however, the historical character of human existence raises this question permanently, while reason is able to recognize partial connections between historical facts, it tries to define the meaning of history by conferring on some of these facts an *absolute value:* particular historical conditions such as place and race or human aims (conquest of nature, the development of the ethical personality, etc.) are raised to the level at which they give a total meaning to the historical process. But then these notions which are used to interpret history, but which are always derived from some one element in historical reality, become so much violence which man offers to history. For as a matter of fact man is not in a position to pass the whole of history in review, and neither as thinker nor as actor does he hold in his hands the magic key to the secret of history.

(5) Today a *religious attempt* at an interpretation of history has to be added to this attempt at a rational knowledge of it. We can detect at work in it a living feeling for the " numinous," for the transcendent in history, as this is attested by the whole history of religion. Man seeks to apprehend the divine working in great historical events, in defeat and victory, collapse and renewal, and also in the happy preservation and extension of an historical heritage (" God was with our fathers ") .

For example, in Germany today a new form of a *religion of history,* a piety based on history, has arisen under the influence of shattering historical events comparable with those of the War of Independence, 1813–15. It contains the following characteristic ideas:

(*a*) God and history, time and eternity flow into one another; the historical hour through which we are actually passing is conceived as the divine *kairos.* Man's deeds in history are in themselves the action of the divine itself;

God is regarded as the " ground " or " power " in history, so that he is present in it.

(*b*) *Secular history becomes sacred history.* The historical moment becomes the moment of salvation. Thus the religion of history does away with the distinction between the action of the Creator and Lord of history on the one hand and God's revelation of salvation on the other. The historical present is transfigured in the eschatological sense as the dawn of a new and perfect age. From this it follows that:

(*c*) The relative opposition of historical periods between the old and the new in history is turned into an eschatological and absolute antithesis between the old age and the new. Thus the knowledge of the *limits* of history as a *whole* disappears, those limits, namely, which no period within history can overpass, and which reduce to relativity all periods of history, great and small alike.

The senseless feature in this religion of history, therefore, lies in the very fact that it refuses to take the historical character of human nature seriously! It is a flight into security, into a state in which it is guaranteed against history, flight into the refuge offered by a moment of unique fulfilment, which yet only *seems* to govern historical occurrences. This religion of history is no longer prepared to accept God's dealings in history as incomprehensible and beyond our disposal. When God is equated with world history the true equation of *man* and history is destroyed.

Yet this religion of history could not have arisen were it not for the question of the meaning and ground of the historical process, which constantly breaks forth from the historical character of human existence. This means, from the Christian point of view, that God appointed the peoples their times and determined the bounds of their habitation " that they might seek God."

(6) *The religion of history raises for the Christian understanding of history this question: how are we to discern God's working in history?*

From what was said above it follows that:

(a) World history is *full of God's working:* there would be no history apart from God's almighty, all-creating and all-determining activity.

(b) The divine rule of the world and of history *has in view sacred history and the consummation of all things* (with an eschatological reference). The meaning of history is, indeed, the coming salvation. Secular history is not sacred history but God guides it towards this, and at the last when it comes to an end, it is *taken up* into sacred history.

(c) The divine working in history is *concealed.* We do not know the details of God's plan for history. It is the *deus absconditus* who meets us in secular history;

(d) But to say this is not to deny that divine power draws near to us in history. God can emerge out of his darkness. There is an existential *divine action in historical events, a historical event which is " for me " or " for us,"* and which concerns me as an individual or a whole society, a nation or a society of nations; as when God binds two persons to one another, saves a man from danger of death, sends to a nation success and victory or a severe defeat. When we bow before such action on God's part, intervening in the storms of history, when we thank and praise God for his wonderful works, this is no mere heathenism, or natural religion of history, any more than — in the case of a harvest festival or grace before meat — when we thank the Creator for the fruits of the earth and the food we eat, we have to do with nature worship. But such historical occurrences coming from God's hand have *not* the import of *salvation.* I have to seek the forgiveness of my sins at

another place, in the Word of the *deus revelatus*. If God
gives a man historical activity, fame and sovereignty, it does
not follow that that man's sins are forgiven.   The victory
of a nation does not carry with it the saving grace of God
but is an historical donation of earthly life.   The downfall of a nation does not mean that God has judged and
rejected it, for he does not take from it his gospel.   Especially is it true that God may act differently at the present
day from the way in which he acted in the past.   The
knowledge of this should make the nations which occupy
a high position in history humble and modest.   " He casts
down the mighty from their seats."   Thus we must reject
all *naïve and fanatical* faith in Providence, which tries to
deduce guarantees of success or salvation from historical
events.

(7) *Everything* which has been said up to this point in
criticism of these attempts at a rational or religious knowledge of God in history presupposes the following decisive
considerations:

(a) *Only a faith which is pledged to the revelation in
salvation of the triune God and has been awakened by this
knows the meaning of history,* the meaning, that is to say,
which God *has given to our sinful and creaturely world
history by the coming of his Kingdom.*

(b) All other knowledge of history on man's part means
a *vague awareness of an indefinite " divine "* element in
history; it can go so far as to assume " that there is a God,"
but it cannot know who and what this God is and how he
feels towards us.   It is a *search for God,* and as such it is to
be honored and taken seriously; but wherever out of man's
own question, which has no answer given within it, man
wants to provide himself with his own answer, this is a form
of *idolatry* which must be rejected.   Only in listening to
the God who reveals himself for our salvation can we come

to know the *answer* to the question about the God of history.

(*c*) Since, however, sacred history makes our time an " interim period " and is not yet itself the consummation, even the Christian knowledge of history has its limits. Whether we are actors or observers we see the interconnection of events only a bit at a time. In so far as we have faith we are raised above the world of history, but at the same time we remain in the place assigned to us in history, and we cannot choose the time in which we are to live. The tension of historical existence consists, therefore, for the Christian in the fact that in virtue of Christ's revelation, as a member of the church he has *a share in the meaning of history as this is displayed in sacred history,* and at the same time *a share in the limitations of human and historical existence.*

6. THE SIGNIFICANCE OF THE CHRISTIAN UNDERSTANDING OF HISTORY FOR THE CHURCH'S TASK IN THE WORLD

(1) *The Christian attitude.* The Christian understanding of history requires and makes possible:

(*a*) *The fear of God,* whose judgments are already powerful and incomprehensible within the realm of history, and the constant awareness of the *transitory nature* of all historical life and action.

(*b*) *The freedom and joy of service in the world, and of a share in the common life of history,* in which we are set as earthly creatures. As Christians we can take upon ourselves our historical existence with all its need and perils in a quite new sense; in the courage which is born of faith and in Christian freedom from the world we receive through our life in Christ *new power to bring our historical existence* to completion. We live our history in the strength of the new creation, before God and for him, since

he is round about us on every side.   We receive a *new vocation to the world,* in which with a sober sense of realities,
but also with utter devotion, we can dedicate ourselves to
historical tasks in the home and family, in our profession
and business, our nation and state.   In spite of its transitory nature this vocation to the world and to historical work
is incumbent on us because the world is and remains God's,
as will be anew attested and confirmed by him at the coming of his Kingdom, and because secular history is being
guided towards the coming of God's Kingdom in its perfection.

(*c*) The attitude of the Christian as he thus accepts
with joy his historical existence is a finite one, and is pre-
eminently one of *waiting in hope*.   All historical reality is
time, and is, therefore, a waiting on the Lord.[10]   This waiting is a condition of constant preparation, knowledge of
the nearness of the end and the suddenness of the Lord's
coming.   But this does not mean that as Christians we are
condemned to historical inactivity.   The time which is
assigned to us is a time of grace which God has granted us
— for repentance, for growth in faith and love; but all this
can take place only within the reality of our historical life
and also as its sanctification.   " The time granted to us is
the time which we have to fill " [11] for it is certain that God
has never cancelled his command as creator that man
should subdue the earth, not even after man fell.   It is the
hope of the Lord's coming and our waiting for the end
which calls us to be stewards of God for the concerns and
labors of this historical period in which we now are.   This
time of waiting is not empty, but it is *full and active
waiting*.

[10] R. Hermann, *on the question of the " christlichen Geschichts-
deutung,"* Wort und Tat, 1936, Vol. 8, p. 228 ff.
[11] R. Hermann, op. cit.

(*d*) This hope, however, always includes a *certainty of victory;* and certainty of victory produces strong endurance and patience. This preserves the Christian in his historical action against losing himself in bitterness, hatred, resentment and excited controversy. But this is the serious danger to which Christianity is exposed today when it is surrounded on all sides by opponents. Such an attitude means defending oneself against the world with the weapons of the world, and it is not the freedom, the patience, and the love to which Christ has called us. In this phase of history we can and ought to endure patiently, and act energetically, in the certainty that Christ is and will be victor.

(2) *Christian influence.* Coupled with this Christian attitude in the period of history still granted to us, there is at the same time the *possibility and the necessity of a Christian influence on the world,* and on great social institutions such as the nation and the state.

Though we repudiate a false optimism about the possibilities of Christian influence on human society, yet the fact remains that: (a) the Christian church *has had and continues to have a formative influence on society and culture,* and that (b) *she ought to and must so act,* because she cannot be shut off from the world but has actually been sent into the world. Such action is a consequence of obedience to the missionary command of Jesus Christ.

Now it is of decisive importance to see that the church does not exercise this formative influence on societies, nations, and cultures by drawing up great cultural and social programs, and by setting up special organizations, to enable her to permeate political and economic life, but by *herself really being a church,* and by binding her members together in the spiritual organization of public worship and prayer to form a *living community.* The fact that such a

community is in the world and the life which it lives in
public worship are of infinitely greater importance for the
" transformation " of the world than all transitory and
time-conditioned programs, and much more important
than all theological criticism of culture and secular life, no
matter with how much enthusiasm the church may give
itself to this. *The fact that the church is there, in the midst
of time and history, is what alters and continues to alter the
world and history,* in so far as the church is faithful to its
charge.   This concealed, though really effective power of
the church is shown clearly by the violent passions of the
anti-Christian movements which are like a fever, with the
aid of which the world wants to drive out its sickness —
that is, the church.   But this cannot be done; for the
church is but the result of the coming of God's Kingdom
into the world by the mission of Jesus Christ, and so it *remains* within time and history right to their end.   All ages
and all forces which dominate the world, whether of a spiritual or a political character, must come to terms with it.
A thousand times declared to be dead, it convicts the false
prophets of lying and wins a new life in spite of its own
weakness.   And in all this its activity reaches out into the
world far beyond the life of the individual Christian.

Both with the proclamation of God's commands and of
redemption the church proclaims *God's sovereignty over
the whole world.*   It seeks to make its way to all peoples
with its message, with its intercession it embraces the needs
and concerns of the whole world.   So it cannot leave the
world to itself; because God loves the world it cannot hand
it over to the demonic powers.

Of course, although certain Christian developments
(e.g., the science of theology, Christian education, the inclusion of the commandment of love in the general morality) arise as a result of the church's presence in history,

there is never a completely Christian state of the world. Every Christian development breaks up again and must be won afresh; the secular forces constantly break through such Christian achievements. The *advancing,* world-influencing church becomes once more a church *rejected by the world.* The Christian church stands today in the midst of this latter process, that of being rejected. Every successful attempt, therefore, to give a Christian form to historical life itself remains *within the historical process, which cannot bring the historical struggle to an end,* but must itself perish. Only the church as it waits in hope understands that any influence which Christianity exerts on various ages or on historical institutions must somehow serve to *prepare the world for its last hour,* for the coming of God's ultimate sovereignty.

(3) *The Christian interpretation of the present.* The following different attitudes to this problem are in principle possible:

(a) A theology which takes a purely transcendent view of the Kingdom of God, and knows only a proclamation of God's Word which is the *same* for *all* times, *denies* that the interpretation of the present is a Christian task.

(b) A *secularized* Christianity, which teaches that political decisions and philosophical ideas as to the nature of the world are the true, or at any rate for the time being the necessary *crystallizations* of the Christian gospel, has its own interpretation of the present time.

But we must neither *subject* the Christian gospel to the present hour nor leave it in the air as *something abstract.* If, however, we are resolved to avoid these two mistakes we have to deal with two *main difficulties:*

A. (i) The transition to the concrete theological statement which interprets the present, always brings with it *some elements of secular historical existence;* these elements are drawn from the connection of this existence with space and time and the life of a particular people; they spring from the distinctive quality of the historical consciousness — for instance, from the breadth of the historical horizon of a definite epoch. This procedure is *necessary*, because we can only form our judgments by starting from the concrete historical position in which we stand. Thus the judgment which the Christian in Germany (with his experience of the present menace of anti-Christian Bolshevism) passes on the present state of things is bound to be different from that of the American or English Christian, who cannot recognize in Bolshevism the great demonic force of the hour, because he has had no historical experience of it as a reality. The *political* view and decision which dominate the situation at any given moment must be regarded as one of the historical elements affecting the Christian interpretation of the future. Even in a theology which lies quite beyond politics and historical realities this is in some sense present, though concealed; for there is no one who does not take some part, be it only by negations, in the political world. Even the person who rejects every political decision within the state system to which he belongs commits himself by that very fact to a decision. It is essential that we should make these elements of political and historical existence openly known as such, instead of *concealing them* under a theology which is too proud to concern itself with anything in this world, and so *letting them continue to operate without hindrance or criticism*.

(ii) Given the same basic attitude as described above in (1) and (2) on the part of Christians, *divergent practical conclusions* can be drawn therefrom, without one being able on that account from the standpoint of one conclusion to condemn the others as unchristian, or to stigmatize the basic attitude as apostasy from Christian discipleship on

account of the conclusion drawn from it (as e.g., in ecclesiastical politics).

(iii) Positively speaking, the task of giving a Christian
interpretation to the present is a special instance of the
Christian task of sanctifying the world in the sphere of
knowledge. The world must not be allowed to fall a prey
to false prophecies or to world views which turn on invest-
ing some particular sphere of reality with absolute value.

It is for us rather to understand each historical present
as it comes in the light of what is at the center of history,
Jesus Christ and the salvation he accomplished once for all;
we do not interpret revelation by means of historical existence but *historical existence by means of revelation.*

This will give us on each occasion first the *Word which
is always the same* and applies to all times and to every
present: namely, that our historical existence is that of
sinful creatures, that every hour in history after Christ
is characterized by the struggle between faith and unbelief,
God's Kingdom and the power of Satan, and so forth. We
cannot avoid the constant repetition of this Christian message concerning the present, and we have no power to
alter it.

B. Second, however, we have to speak the *concrete Word*
of Christian interpretation which *changes with each change
in historical existence.* This should demonstrate how, at
the present hour, man and human society have become
apostate from the sovereignty of God. The decision at
which faith must actually arrive in face of the present
menace of Antichrist cannot be wholly uniform throughout the whole of Christendom, inasmuch as the individual
churches find themselves in different situations. It will
become more uniform the more the total position of ecumenical Christianity shows the same features prevailing
everywhere (and there is no doubt that this is coming

more and more to be the case). But this decision is also dependent on God's awakening within the church the prophetic spirit in men who see more than "average Christians," who have not yet attained their majority in Christ, are able to see. It is a heavy trial for the church when she has to go without the prophetic interpretation of history by the power of the Spirit, as the seer John or Luther gave it to the church of their time. This gift is also connected with a particular need and a particular situation, and does not claim to reveal in one comprehensive survey the whole divine plan of history.[12] This present-day type of apostasy in its prevailing form may be recognized at present as follows:

(i) By the progressive *dissolution* of all *Christian* influence upon culture and social institutions and of any Christian standards for them;

(ii) By the extreme development of the general secular spirit into something *anti-Christian,* to be seen at work partly in a violent effort to destroy the church of Christ and partly in the detachment of the church from public life. This anti-Christian movement has a religious basis and wants to substitute its own form of worship for the church of Christ. It is, therefore, to be looked upon as an *opposition* church.

(iii) But behind this anti-Christian religion and this opposition church stands the imperious necessity of finding *basic institutions and norms* which will be simple, universally intelligible, and within the experience of *everyone,* so that they will be able to bind man to man and overcome our present chaotic situation in the social and ethical sphere. This need and the demand which it arouses — which have led in part to definite *Renaissance movements* (a renewal of the values of earlier periods,

12 Cf. the Seven Epistles of the Apocalypse and Luther's interpretation of the Papacy as Antichrist.

return to an historical source), and in part to a *new, irrational law of nature* — will still remain, even when such demonic forces as a Bolshevist or a nationalist religion have been exposed or successfully opposed.

So that the question which the church addresses to the present hour leads us back to a *question which the present hour addresses to the church:*

If it be true that new world views, myths and religions are unable to restore order to a world that is out of joint, because they cannot lead to the true God, *can the church once more assure the leadership of mankind, and bind our ruined society into a coherent whole,* since the church claims to know God's commandment and to live in the coming Kingdom of God as a present fact?

Though this question may be wrongly formulated, though it may show a misunderstanding of the church's specific task, yet it does suggest that the tremendous *claim* of the church must be combined with a life which *heals* because it *sanctifies.*

Our criticism of the demonic forces of the present ends in a criticism of the church. Only so long as this is what happens is the Christian interpretation of the present a sincere one, and able to ward off the dangers of Christian resentment and Christian pharisaism. We must distinguish between the *false significance* attached to a reality and the reality itself. The rejection of Marxism as demonic must not make us overlook the sick and ruined condition of society out of which this illusion arose; so the rejection of nationalism as demonic must not make us despise the people, the nation and the state, our love to them and our responsibility for them so that we exclude them from the Christian account of the world. Above all we must keep in mind the danger that the Christian exposure of these demonic forces may be made into a formula to be regularly employed whenever we want to find a dis-

guise for our own political decision against a political system and a political idea.

Since as Christians we stand within our several nations,
it is our duty to preserve the " Christian understanding
of history " in such a form that we shall not only oppose
the demonic powers at work in national messianism, but
shall enter with sympathy into the problems and the needs
of millions of our fellow men who ask in all simplicity and
seriousness about the fate and the future of their people
and country. For this question is involved in the fact that
human nature exists under the specific form of peoples and
nations. Simply to expose the demonic aspect of nationalism does not solve this problem because this has nothing to
do with it. It is a datum of our existence as creatures.
Only when we make *their* question *our own,* when we attempt to answer the question raised by that historical existence which we have *in common with them* by means of that
relation with God which has been granted to us, shall we
save the peoples from falling victims to a nationalistic meta-
physic or national messianism. The merely negative criticism of heresies and powers of deception may *condemn,*
but it does not help. With nations as with individuals to
confine oneself to passing judgment means renouncing the
cure of souls.

Heresy and the work of the demons are not to be found
in the question a nation asks when it seeks to learn what
meaning attaches to its peculiar existence and what its
future will be like — there is as little " heathenism " or
" polytheism " in this as when the individual inquires
into his existence and his destiny. They are to be found
rather in man's attempt to answer these questions of his
national life without God, or by using him for his own ends,
for in so doing he deifies his own origin or the future for
which he looks for his nation.

THE KINGDOM OF GOD AND HISTORY

by

Christopher Dawson

THE KINGDOM OF GOD AND HISTORY

THE development of a historical sense — a distinct consciousness of the essential characteristics of different ages
and civilizations — is a relatively recent achievement; in
fact it hardly existed before the nineteenth century. It is
above all the product of the Romantic movement which
first taught men to respect the diversity of human life, and
to regard culture not as an abstract ideal but as the vital
product of an organic social tradition. No doubt, as
Nietzsche pointed out, the acquisition of this sixth sense is
not all pure gain, since it involves the loss of that noble self-
sufficiency and maturity in which the great ages of civilization culminate — " the moment of smooth sea and halcyon
self-sufficiency, the goldenness and coldness which all
things show that have perfected themselves." It was rendered possible only by the " democratic mingling of classes
and races " which is characteristic of modern European
civilization. " Owing to this mingling the past of every
form and mode of life and of cultures which were formerly
juxtaposed with or superimposed on one another flow forth
into us," so that " we have secret access everywhere such as a
noble age never had; we have access above all to the laby-
rinth of imperfect civilizations and to every form of semi-
barbarity that has at any time existed on earth." [1]

Yet it is impossible to believe that the vast widening of
the range and scope of consciousness that the historical
sense has brought to the human race is an ignoble thing,
as Nietzsche would have us believe. It is as though man

[1] F. Nietzsche, *Beyond Good and Evil*, 224.

had at last climbed from the desert and the forest and the fertile plain on to the bare mountain slopes whence he can look back and see the course of his journey and the whole extent of his kingdom. And to the Christian, at least, this widening vision and these far horizons should bring not doubt and disillusionment, but a firmer faith in the divine power that has guided him and a stronger desire for the divine kingdom which is the journey's end.

It is in fact through Christianity above all that man first acquired that sense of a unity and a purpose in history without which the spectacle of the unending change becomes meaningless and oppressive.

" The rational soul," writes Marcus Aurelius, " traverses the whole universe and the surrounding void, and surveys its form, and it extends itself with the infinity of time and embraces and comprehends the periodical revolutions of all things, and it comprehends that those who come after us will see nothing new, nor have those before us seen anything more, but in a manner he who is forty years old, if he has any understanding at all has seen by virtue of the uniformity that prevails all things that have been or that will be." [2]

This denial of the significance of history is the rule rather than the exception among philosophers and religious teachers throughout the ages from India to Greece and from China to Northern Europe. Even Nietzsche, who grew up in the tradition of the modern historical movement and himself possessed so delicate and profound a historical sense, could not escape the terrifying vision of *The Return of All Things*, even though it seemed to nullify his own evolutionary gospel of the superman. " Behold," he wrote, " this moment. Two roads meet here and none has ever reached their end. . . ." " From this gate-

[2] *Marcus Aurelius*, 11:1. Trans. G. Long.

way a long eternal road runs back: behind us lies an eternity. Must not all things that *can* run have run this road? Must not all that can happen have already happened, have already been done and passed through? And if all has already been, what . . . of this moment? Must not this gateway also have been before? And are not all things knotted together in such a way that this moment draws after it all that is to come, and therefore also itself? For all that can run — even in this long road behind, must run it yet again.

" And this slow spider that crawls in the moonlight and this moonlight itself, and you and I whispering together in the gateway, must we not all have been before?

" And must we not come again and run that other long road before us — that long shadowy road — must we not return eternally? " [3]

As St. Augustine said,[4] it is only by Christ the Straight Way that we are delivered from the nightmare of these eternal cycles which seem to exercise a strange fascination over the human mind in any age and clime.

Nevertheless, Christianity does not itself create the historical sense. It only supplies the metaphysical and theological setting for history and an attempt to create a theory of history from the data of revealed truth alone will give us not a history but a theodicy like St. Augustine's City of God or the *Praeparatio Evangelica* of Eusebius. The modern historical consciousness is the fruit of Christian tradition and Christian culture but not of these alone. It also owes much to humanism which taught the European mind to study the achievements of ancient civilization and to value human nature for its own sake. And it was the contact and conflict of these two traditions and ideals —

[3] *Also Sprach Zarathustra*, 30:2:2.
[4] *de Civ. Dei*, 12:20.

Christianity and humanism — classical and mediaeval culture — that found expression in the Romantic movement
in which the modern historical sense first attained full consciousness. For it was only then and thus that the human
mind realized that a culture forms an organic unity with
its own social traditions and its own spiritual ideals, and
that consequently we cannot understand the past by applying the standards and values of our own age and civilization to it, but only by relating historical facts to the social
tradition to which they belong and by using the spiritual
beliefs and the moral and intellectual values of that tradition as the key to their interpretation.

Hence the essence of history is not to be found in facts
but in traditions. The pure fact is not as such historical.
It only becomes historical when it can be brought into
relation with a social tradition so that it is seen as part of
an organic whole. A visitor from another planet who
witnessed the Battle of Hastings would possess far greater
knowledge of the facts than any modern historian, yet
this knowledge would not be historical for lack of any
tradition to which it could be related; whereas the child
who says " William the Conqueror 1066 " has already made
his atom of knowledge an historical fact by relating it to
a national tradition and placing it in the time-series of
Christian culture.

Wherever a social tradition exists, however small and
unimportant may be the society which is its vehicle, the
possibility of history exists. It is true that many societies
fail to realize this possibility, or realize it only in an un-
scientific or legendary form, but on the other hand this
legendary element is never entirely absent from social
tradition, and even the most civilized society has its national legend or myth, of which the scientific historian is
often an unconscious apologist. No doubt it is the ideal of

the modern historian to transcend the tradition of his own society and to see history as one and universal, but in fact such a universal history does not exist. There is as yet no history of humanity, since humanity is not an organized society with a common tradition or a common social consciousness. All the attempts that have hitherto been made to write a world history have been in fact attempts to interpret one tradition in terms of another, attempts to extend the intellectual hegemony of a dominant culture by subordinating to it all the events of other cultures that come within the observer's range of vision. The more learned and conscientious a historian is, the more conscious he is of the relativity of his knowledge, and the more ready he is to treat the culture that he is studying as an end in itself, an autonomous world which follows its own laws and owes no allegiance to the standards and ideals of another civilization. For history deals with civilizations and cultures rather than civilization, with the development of particular societies and not with the progress of humanity.

Consequently if we rely on history alone we can never hope to transcend the sphere of relativity; it is only in religion and metaphysics that we can find truths that claim absolute and eternal validity. But as we have said, non-Christian and pre-Christian philosophy tend to solve the problem of history by a radical denial of its significance. The world of true Being which is man's spiritual home is the world that knows no change. The world of time and change is the material world from which man must escape if he would be saved. For all the works of men and the rise and fall of kingdoms are but the fruits of ignorance and lust — *mala vitae cupido* — and even the masters of the world must recognize in the end the vanity of their labors like the great Shogun Hideyoshi who wrote on his deathbed:

> Alas, as the grass I fade
> As the dew I vanish
> Even Osaka Castle
> Is a dream within a dream.

Yet even the religion that denies the significance of history is itself a part of history and it can only survive in so far as it embodies itself in a social tradition and thus " makes history." The spiritual experience from which a religion receives its initial impetus — like the contemplation of Buddha under the Bo tree or Mohammed's vision in the cavern on Mt. Hira — may seem as completely divested of historical and social reference as any human experience can be. Yet as soon as the teacher comes down among men and his followers begin to put his teachings into practice a tradition is formed which comes into contact with other social traditions and embraces them or is absorbed by them, until its very nature seems to be changed by this chemistry of history. Thus we see Buddhism passing from India to Central Asia and China, and from China to Korea and Japan and again to Ceylon and Burma and Siam. We see it taking different forms in different cultures and at the same time changing the cultures themselves, while all the while the religion itself ignores historical change and remains with its gaze averted from life, absorbed in the contemplation of Nirvana.

Now at first sight it may seem that this is true of Christianity; that it also has been absorbed against its will in the stream of historical change while its attention has been concentrated on eternal truths and its hopes fixed on eternal life. It is easy to find examples in Christianity of world flight and world denial no less extreme than that of the Indian sannyasi: the fathers of the desert, St. Simeon on his pillar, Thomas à Kempis in his cell and the countless pious Christians of every age and country who have regarded this life as an exile in the vale of tears and have orientated their whole existence towards death and immortality. In fact the current criticism of Christianity is based on this conception and the communist sneer about " pie in sky when you die " is merely a crude and malicious statement of what has always been an essential element of the Christian faith and one which is nowhere more prominent than in the gospel itself.

Nevertheless this is only one side of the Christian view of life, for Christianity has always possessed an organic relation to history which distinguishes it from the great Oriental religions and philosophies. Christianity can never ignore history because the Christian revelation is essentially historical and the truths of faith are inseparably connected with historical events. The sacred Scriptures of our religion are not made up of expositions of metaphysical doctrines like the Vedanta, they form a *sacred history*, the record of God's dealings with the human race from the creation of man to the creation of the church. And the whole of this history finds its center in the life of a historic personality who is not merely a moral teacher or even an inspired hierophant of divine truth, but God made man, the Savior and restorer of the human race, from whom and in whom humanity acquires a new life and a new principle of unity.

Thus the Christian faith leaves no room for the relativism of a merely historical philosophy. For here at one moment of time and space there occurs an event of absolute value and incomparable significance for all times and all peoples. Amid the diversity and discontinuity of human civilizations and traditions there appears One who is one and the same for all men and for all ages: in whom all the races and traditions of man find their common center.

Yet on the other hand the incarnation does not involve

any denial of the significance of history such as we find in the Gnostic and Manichaean heresies. It is itself in a sense the fruit of history, since it is the culminating point of one tradition, and the starting point of another. The appeal to tradition is one of the most characteristic features of the gospel. The New Testament opens with "the book of the generation of Jesus Christ the son of David, the son of Abraham," and the first preaching of the apostles starts with an appeal to a tradition that goes back to Ur of the Chaldeans and the earliest origins of the Hebrew people.

Thus, the Christian church possessed its own history, which was a continuation of the history of the chosen people, and this history had its own autonomous development which was independent of the currents of secular history. We have the age of the apostles and the age of the martyrs and the age of the fathers, each of them built on the same foundations and contributing its part to the building up of the City of God.

The chief problem, therefore, which we have to study is that of the relations between this sacred tradition and the other countless traditions that make up human history. For Christianity, no less than the other world religions, has entered the stream of historical change and has passed from one race to another, from civilization to barbarism and from barbarism to civilization. Men of different periods with different historical backgrounds and different national or racial traditions all belong to the all-embracing tradition of the Christian church. We have Hellenistic Christians and Byzantine Christians, Romans and Syrians, Mediaeval Christians and Renaissance Christians, seventeenth century Spaniards and nineteenth century Englishmen. Are these differences of culture and race accidental and ephemeral — details that have no relevance to the Christian view of life and the Christian interpretation of history? Or are they also of spiritual significance as elements in the divine plan and forms through which the providential purpose of God in history is manifested?

Now from the early Christian point of view, at least, it would seem that the whole significance of history was entirely comprised in that sacred tradition of which we have spoken. The key to history — the mystery of the ages — was to be found in the tradition of the chosen people and the sacred community, and outside that tradition among the Gentiles and the kingdoms of men there is a realm of endless strife and confusion, a succession of empires founded by war and violence and ending in blood and ruin. The Kingdom of God is not the work of man and does not emerge by a natural law of progress from the course of human history. It makes a violent irruption into history and confounds the work of man, like the stone hewn from the mountain without human agency which crushes the image of the four world empires into dust.

One of the most striking features of the Christian tradition is, in fact, its historical dualism: in the Old Testament the opposition between the chosen people and the Gentiles; in the New, the opposition between the church and the world — in the Augustinian theodicy, the two cities, Jerusalem and Babylon — the community of charity and the community of self-will. Yet this dualism is never an absolute one. Even the Old Testament, in spite of its insistence in the unique privilege of Israel as the exclusive bearer of the divine promise, also recognizes the hand of God in the history of the Gentiles. Even the powers that seem most hostile to the people of God are the instrument by which God works out his purpose. This is shown most remarkably in the Isaianic prophecy with regard to Cyrus, for here a Gentile ruler is addressed by the messianic title as chosen and anointed by God to do his will and to deliver his people. No doubt here and elsewhere the divine action in history always has a direct reference to the fortunes of the people of God. But the converse is also true, for God's dealings with his people are of profound significance for the future of the Gentiles. In the end the Holy City will be the resort of all peoples; the Gentiles will bring their riches into it, and from it there will go forth the law of justice and grace to all the nations of the earth.

And in the New Testament there is a still further recognition of a limited but intrinsic value in the social order and social traditions that lie outside the dispensation of grace. Even the pagan state is God's servant in so far as it is the guardian of order and the administrator of justice. And in the higher sphere of grace, the passing of the old racial restrictions and the opening of the Kingdom to all nations involved at least in principle the consecration of every nation and of every social tradition in so far as they were not corrupted by sin. And so we have the reception into the church of Greek philosophy and scholarship, and of Roman law and leadership, until the whole civilized world found itself Christian. The vital thing was not the conversion of the Empire and the union of church and state, but the gradual penetration of culture by the Christian tradition, until that tradition embraced the whole of the life of Western man in all its historic diversity and left no human activity and no social tradition unconsecrated.

With this coming in of the nations and the establishment of the Kingdom of Christ among the Gentiles the Christian interpretation of prophecy seemed to have been fulfilled. From the time of St. Augustine Christian millenniarism was generally abandoned and the messianic kingdom was identified with the triumph of the church — " *ecclesia et nunc est regnum Christi regnumque coelorum.*" It seemed to the men of that age witnessing the fall of the Empire and the ruin of civilization that nothing remained to be accomplished except the last things. Consequently the Christian interpretation of history became mainly retrospective, and the present and the future of man's attention were concentrated not on history but on the end of history which seemed close at hand.

But with the passing of ages and the birth of new nations and new forms of culture, new problems presented themselves to the Christian conscience. The Augustinian theology with its intense realization of the inherited burden of evil which weighs down the human race and its conception of divine grace as a supernatural power which renews human nature and changes the course of history, continued to inspire the mediaeval outlook, and the mediaeval interpretation of history is still based on the Augustinian conception of the two cities. But whereas St. Augustine presents this opposition primarily as a conflict between the Christian church and the heathen world, the Middle Ages saw it above all as a struggle between the forces of good and evil within Christian society. The reform of the church, the restoration of moral order, and the establishment of social justice — these were the vital problems that occupied the mind of mediaeval Christendom from the tenth century onwards; and the whole movement of reform from the time of St. Odo of Cluny to that of St. Bernard and Otto of Freising was consciously based on an interpretation of history which applied the Augustinian concept of the two cities to the contemporary crisis between church and state or rather between the religious and secular forces that were at war within the Christian community. This neo-Augustinian view of history finds its most direct expression in the writings of Odo of Cluny in the tenth century, Bonizo of Sutri in the eleventh and

Otto of Freising in the twelfth, but it also inspired some of the ablest partisans of the Empire such as the author of the treatise *De Unitate Ecclesiae conservanda.* For the mediaeval empire and indeed the mediaeval kingship were not regarded by their supporters as secular institutions in our sense of the word. They were the leaders of the Christian people and the defenders of the Christian faith, and it was to them rather than to the papacy and the priesthood that the government of Christendom as an historical " temporal " order had been committed by God.

This tradition of Christian imperialism was not destroyed by the victory of the papacy over the Empire. In fact it found its most remarkable expression in the fourteenth century in Dante's theory of the providential mission of the Roman Empire as the society through which the human race would realize its potential unity and attain universal peace, and of the particular vocation of the messianic prince the mystical DVX who would be the savior of Italy and the reformer of the church. Here for the first time we have a Christian interpretation of history which looks beyond the sacred Judaeo-Christian tradition and admits the independent value and significance of the secular tradition of culture. There are in fact two independent but parallel dispensations — the dispensation of grace which is represented by the church and the natural dispensation by which humanity attains its rational end by the agency of the Roman people, which was ordained by nature and elected by God for universal empire.

Thus while on the one hand Dante's interpretation of history looks back to the mediaeval tradition of the Holy Roman Empire and the Augustinian ideal of the City of God, on the other hand it looks forward to the humanism of the Renaissance and the modern liberal ideal of universal peace as well as the modern nationalist ideal of the historical mission of a particular people and state. And this idea of a predestined correspondence between the secular tradition of human civilization embodied in the Roman Empire and the religious tradition of supernatural truth embodied in the catholic church finds its philosophical basis in the Thomist doctrine of the concordance of nature and grace. If it had been adopted by Thomism as the basis of the interpretation of history, it might well have developed with the growth of historical knowledge into a really catholic philosophy of history in which the different national traditions were shown, on the analogy of that of Rome, as contributing each according to its own mission and its natural aptitudes towards the building up of a Christian civilization. Actually, however, Dante's attachment to the dying cause of Ghibelline imperialism prevented his philosophy from exercising any wide influence on catholic thought. It remained an impressive but eccentric witness to the universalism of mediaeval thought and the lost spiritual unity of mediaeval culture.

For the close of the Middle Ages was marked by the great religious revolution which destroyed the unity of Western Christendom and divided the peoples of Europe by the strife of sects and the conflict of opposing religious traditions. There was no longer one common Catholic faith and consequently there was no longer a common sacred tradition or a common interpretation of history. It is true that the Reformers inherited far more from the Middle Ages than they themselves realized and this was particularly the case with regard to the interpretation of history. Their conception of history, no less than that of the Middle Ages, is based on the Bible and St. Augustine, and the Augustinian scheme of world history based on the opposition and conflict of the two cities had as great an influence on Luther and Calvin and the seventeenth century Puritan divines as it had on the Catholic reformers five centuries earlier.

Nevertheless the catholic interpretation of history is organically related to the catholic conception of the nature and office of the church, and in so far as Protestantism formed a new conception of the church, it ultimately involved a new interpretation of history. Thus already, long before the emergence of the new schools of Biblical criticism and ecclesiastical history that have so profoundly affected the modern Protestant attitude to the catholic tradition, a divergence between the Catholic and Protestant interpretations of history is plainly visible.

At first sight the difference between sixteenth century Catholicism and Protestantism is the difference between the traditional and the revolutionary conceptions of Christianity and of the church. To the Catholic the church was the Kingdom of God on earth — *in via* — the supernatural society through which and in which alone humanity could realize its true end. It was a visible society with its own law and constitution which possessed divine and indefectible authority. It remained through the ages one and the same, like a city set on a hill, plain for all men to see, handing on from generation to generation the same deposit of faith and the same mandate of authority which it had received from its divine Founder and which it would retain whole and intact until the end of time. The Reformers, on the other hand, while maintaining a similar conception of the church as the community through which God's purpose towards the human race is realized, refused to identify this divine society with the actual visible hierarchical church, as known to history. Against the catholic view of the church as the visible City of God, they set the apocalyptic vision of an apostate church, a harlot drunk with the blood of the saints, sitting on the seven hills and intoxicating the nations with her splendor and her evil enchantments. The true church was not this second Babylon, but the society of the elect, the hidden saints who followed the teaching of the Bible rather than of the hierarchy and who were to be found among the so-called heretics — Hussites, Wycliffites, Waldensians and the rest, rather than among the servants of the official institutional church.

The result of this revolutionary attitude to the historic church was a revolutionary, catastrophic, apocalyptic and discontinuous view of history. As Calvin writes, the history of the church is a series of resurrections. Again and again the church becomes corrupt, the Word is no longer preached, life seems extinct, until God once more sends forth prophets and teachers to bear witness to the truth and to reveal the evangelical doctrine in its pristine purity. Thus the Reformation may be compared to the Renaissance since it was an attempt to go back behind the Middle Ages, to wipe out a thousand years of historical development and to restore the Christian religion to its primitive " classical " form. Yet on the other hand this return to the past brought the Protestant mind into fresh contact with the Jewish and apocalyptic sources of the Christian view of history, so that the Reformation led to an increased emphasis on the Hebraic, prophetic and apocalyptic elements in the Christian tradition as against the Hellenic, patristic and metaphysical elements that were so strongly represented alike in patristic orthodoxy and in mediaeval Catholicism.

Hence we find two tendencies in Protestant thought which find their extreme expression respectively in Socinianism and millenniarism. One represents the attempt to strip off all accretions, to separate religion from history and to recover the pure timeless essence of Christianity.

The other represents a crude and vehement reassertion of the historical time-element in Christianity and an attempt to strip it of all its non-Jewish, mystical, philosophical, and theological elements. The resultant type of religion was marked by some of the worst excesses of fanaticism and irrationality, yet on the other hand it was intensely social in spirit, as we see, for example, in the case of the Anabaptists, and it made an earnest, if one-sided and over-simplified, effort to provide a Christian interpretation of history.

But though these two tendencies seem hostile to one another, they were not in fact mutually exclusive. For example, John Milton could be at the same time a millenniarist and a Socinian, and eighteenth century Unitarians, such as Priestley, who seem to represent the Socinian type of Protestantism in an almost pure state, acquired from the opposite tradition a kind of secularized millenniarism which found expression in the doctrine of progress. The development of this rationalized theology and of this secularized millenniarism, whether in its revolutionary-socialistic or revolutionary-liberal forms (but especially the latter) is of central importance for the understanding of modern culture. It was in fact a new reformation, which attempted to rationalize and spiritualize religion in an even more complete and drastic way than the first Reformation had done, but which ended in emptying Christianity of all supernatural elements and interpreting history as the progressive development of an immanent principle.

Thus it is not only the materialistic interpretation of history but the idealistic interpretation as well which is irreconcilable with the traditional Christian view, since it eliminates that sense of divine otherness and transcendence, that sense of divine judgment and divine grace which are the very essence of the Christian attitude to history. This holds true of Protestantism as well as of Catholicism. Nevertheless it must be admitted that the clash is much sharper and more painful in the case of the latter. Partly, no doubt, because the great idealist thinkers, such as Kant, were themselves men of Protestant origin who had preserved a strong Protestant ethos, it has been possible for Protestants to accept the idealist interpretation of history without any serious conflict, and in the same way it was on Protestant rather than on catholic foundations that the new liberal theology of immanence developed itself.

Catholicism, on the other hand, showed little sympathy to the idealist movement which it tended to regard as an external and non-religious force. Its attitude to history was at once more traditionalist and more realist than that of Protestantism and it did not readily accept the idea of an inevitable law of progress which was accepted by both liberal and Protestant idealists as the background of their thought and the basic principle of their interpretation of history. Consequently there is a sharp contrast between the catholic and the liberal-idealist philosophies such as hardly exists in the Protestant world. As Croce brings out so clearly in his *History of Europe in the Nineteenth Century*, it is not a conflict between religion and science or religion and philosophy, but between two rival creeds, based on an irreconcilable opposition of principles and resulting in a completely different view of the world. For, as Croce again points out, the idealist conceptions of monism, immanence and self-determination are the negation of the principles of divine transcendence, divine revelation, and divine authority on which the catholic view of God and man, of creation and history and the end of history is based.

Hence the opposition between liberalism and catholicism is not due, as the vulgar simplification would have it, to the " reactionary " tendencies of the latter but to the necessity of safeguarding the absolute Christian values, both in the theological and the historical spheres. For if Christianity is the religion of the incarnation, and if the Christian interpretation of history depends on the continuation and extension of the incarnation in the life of the church, Catholicism differs from other forms of Christianity in representing this incarnational principle in a fuller, more concrete, and more organic sense. As the Christian faith in Christ is faith in a real historical person, not an abstract ideal, so the catholic faith in the church is faith in a real historic society, not an invisible communion of saints or a spiritual union of Christians who are divided into a number of religious groups and sects. And this historic society is not merely the custodian of the sacred Scriptures and a teacher of Christian morality. It is the bearer of a living tradition which unites the present and the past, the living and the dead, in one great spiritual community which transcends all the limited communities of race and nation and state. Hence it is not enough for the catholic to believe in the Word as contained in the sacred Scriptures, it is not even enough to accept the historic faith as embodied in the creeds and interpreted by catholic theology, it is necessary for him to be incorporated as a cell in the living organism of the divine society and to enter into communion with the historic reality of the sacred tradition. Thus to the student who considers Catholicism as an intellectual system embodied in theological treatises, Catholicism may seem far more legalist and intellectualist than Protestantism which emphasizes so strongly the personal and moral-emotional sides of religion, but the sociologist who studies it in its historical and social reality will soon understand the incomparable importance for Catholicism of tradition which makes the individual a member of an historic society and a spiritual *civilization* and which influences his life and thought consciously and unconsciously in a thousand different ways.

Now the recognition of this tradition as the organ of the Spirit of God in the world and the living witness to the supernatural action of God on humanity is central to the catholic understanding and interpretation of history. But so tremendous a claim involves a challenge to the whole secular view of history which is tending to become the faith of the modern world. In spite of the differences and contradictions between the progressive idealism of liberalism and the catastrophic materialism of communism all of them agree in their insistence on the immanence and autonomy of human civilization and on the secular community as the ultimate social reality. Alike to the liberal and to the communist the catholic tradition stands condemned as " reactionary " not merely for the accidental reason that it has been associated with the political and social order of the past, but because it sets the divine values of divine faith and charity and eternal life above the human values — political liberty, social order, economic prosperity, scientific truth — and orientates human life and history towards a supernatural and super-historical end. And since the modern society is everywhere tending towards ideological uniformity which will leave no room for the private worlds of the old bourgeois culture, the contradiction between secularism and catholicism is likely to express itself in open conflict and persecution. No doubt the prospect of such a conflict is highly distasteful to the modern bourgeois mind, even when it is Christian. The liberal optimism which has been so characteristic of Anglo-Saxon religious thought during the last half century led men to believe that the days of persecution were over and that all men of goodwill would agree to set aside their differences of opinion and unite to combat the evils that were universally condemned — vice and squalor and ignorance. But from the standpoint of the Christian interpretation of history there is no ground for such hopes. Christ came not to bring peace but a sword, and the Kingdom of God comes not by the elimination of conflict but through an increasing opposition and tension between the church and the world. The conflict between the two cities is as old as humanity and must endure to the end of time. And though the church may meet with ages of prosperity, and her enemies may fail and the powers of the world may submit to her sway, these things are no criterion of success. She wins not by majorities but by martyrs and the cross is her victory.

Thus in comparison with the optimism of liberalism the Christian view of life and the Christian interpretation of history are profoundly tragic. The true progress of history is a mystery which is fulfilled in failure and suffering and which will only be revealed at the end of time. The victory that overcomes the world is not success but faith and it is only the eye of faith that understands the true value of history.

Viewing history from this standpoint the Christian will not be confident in success or despondent in failure. " For when you shall hear of wars and rumors of wars be not afraid, for the end is not yet." None knows where Europe is going and there is no law of history by which we can predict the future. Nor is the future in our own hands, for the world is ruled by powers that it does not know, and the men who appear to be the makers of history are in reality its creatures. But the portion of the church is not like these. She has been the guest and the exile, the mistress and the martyr, of nations and civilizations and has survived them all. And in every age and among every people it is her mission to carry on the work of divine restoration and regeneration, which is the true end of history.